MW01594901

Hometown Girl

Hometown Girl

Minta Cypert & Rick Cypert

INFUSIONMEDIA

Lincoln, Nebraska

since 1994

© 2013 Cypert L.L.C.

Except for brief quotes used in reviews, no part of this book may be reproduced, stored in a retrieval system, or transmitted in any form by any means, including mechanical, electronic, photocopying, recording, or otherwise, without prior written permission of the copyright holder.

Infusionmedia
140 North 8th Street #214 The Apothecary
Lincoln, NE 68508-1353 USA
www.infusionmediadesign.com

Printed in the United States

10 9 8 7 6 5 4 3 2 1
First Edition

ISBN: 978-0-9888122-6-0

Library of Congress Control Number: 2013952598

All terms mentioned in this book that are known to be trademarks or service marks have been appropriately capitalized or otherwise specially treated; use of a term in this book should not be regarded as affecting the validity of any trademark or service mark.

Cover photo: Minta Cypert.
Frontispiece: Minta and Walter Cypert.
All photos provided by the authors. Photographers' names are noted when known.

Dedicated to the citizens of Throckmorton and Throckmorton County,
my students, and fellow educators:
from a grateful hometown girl

Contents

Preface

Minta

FIFTY YEARS after his birth, my younger son and I are in the delivery room of our local hospital. The delivery room and the operating room next door now serve as a dual emergency room, and my son is stretched out on a gurney, pale and shivering. After a day's drive from Nebraska where he lives, he arrived in our hometown, where he shortly began throwing up. We do not know if the sickness has been caused by a virus or a bad grilled chicken sandwich he consumed en route. Whatever it is, he asked me to come with him to the hospital. My doctor, now his doctor, orders an injection after my son does not manage to keep down a pill the nurse gave him. He begins shivering violently, and the nurse takes a blanket from a heated cabinet with which to cover him. He settles a bit, and I look around the green tiled room, wondering how many mothers and their grown children have revisited the hospital delivery room where they first saw each other.

"You know," I say to him, "this is the room where you were born."

He looks over at me with a faint grin.

"I hope it's not the room where I go out," he says.

He is feeling better.

Nonetheless, I think about what he said and remember the room at the farmhouse where I was born, where my mother and sister and I spent plenty more time together, and the room at the house in town where my grandmother died, and the parlor where she lay in state. Those rooms served many purposes too for life and for death.

We started this book, my younger son and I, because I had always planned to write about my teaching and because he can ask more questions than just about anyone I know. He is also persistent, determined, and, as one of his primary school teachers recorded on his report card, "bossy." I guess he came by it honestly. As a child, my future husband, Walter, had his way as well. His cousins liked to report that they never knew when they arrived at the farm whether they would find his mother, Edith, sitting on the kitchen floor with her skirt tacked down by her impish son who had discovered a new game to play. I probably provided the same leeway to Rick. So when he told me we needed to write this book, I knew that we would.

* * *

Rick

I LEARNED pretty early to listen to my elders. As a child I went sailing through a room, headed for the back door, ignoring the two old ladies visiting my maternal grandmother. One of these senior citizens, if not spry, was quick and caught my scrawny neck with the hook of her cane before I escaped, pulling me back in front of her chair.

"Do you not stop and speak to visitors?" she asked.

"Yes, ma'am," I croaked. "Hello. How are you?"

After I greeted her companion, she smiled and released my neck from the cane. I stood there rather stupidly gawking, not sure what to do next.

"Weren't you on your way out to play?" she asked.

I nodded.

"Well, be on your way, then," she replied.

Slowly I backed away, warily watching that cane. Although I did not realize it, I had been jerked into some kind of new awareness: older people were potentially dangerous and definitely worth paying attention to.

So I did.

Growing up in my hometown, in my mother's hometown, when the neighborhood kids were not available to play, I would visit those who were available: mostly retired, sometimes sitting on the front porch, or in front of a television, or working in their yard or garden—some of these senior citizens were related to me, some not. What stories I heard, what conversations I had. And all or most of these I would report back to my mother or father, incredulous that they already knew the plot and the characters. Where had they gotten this information?

My curiosity led me to apply, as a teenager, for a job at the local newspaper, where I learned reporting and photography. So, as my mother indicates about this book, she did not have a chance. In my defense, though, she had already been at it—spending long hours with her grandfather, interviewing him about his younger years, collecting family stories, learning her hometown. Later she began writing down her memories from teaching—nearly forty years' worth—and naming names. Oh, not to embarrass anyone, but my mother intends to celebrate her hometown, as much as her life, in this book, and the names of individuals, which might mean nothing to many readers, surely provide a level of verisimilitude and a nod to the individual's importance. Once I found my mother's manuscripts I knew it was time for the two of us to sit down together for more conversations. Oh, what conversations. Is there anything more pleasing than realizing that you have asked a question to someone that has released a memory long tucked away?

✳ ✳ ✳

More pleasing than asking the question is supplying the answer, and in supplying the answer reliving a moment. More pleasing than asking the question is finding the answer, by persistence, in letters, old photographs, or yearbooks, or through sudden realization after letting the question sit for a time. More pleasing than asking the question is connecting the stories that emerge, looking for patterns among them, figuring out a way forward.

CHAPTER ONE

From Whence I Come and Where I Am

M Y younger son and I step out of the church into a cold December night carrying two potted poinsettias that helped decorate the sanctuary up through the Christmas Eve communion service. One I gave in memory of my husband, now deceased sixteen years, the other in memory of my mother, who died thirty-eight years ago. We drive past houses, some dark and silent, others festively lit with Christmas lights, to the northeast corner of town, up an incline to the cemetery. Crossing between the stone gate columns, we watch for our turn, passing the headstones of friends and family, until we pull alongside the Parmenter family plot. My husband never liked flowers on graves, so his plant we leave in the back of the car. My son takes a shovel and begins digging a small, round hole in front of my mother's headstone. When at last he is satisfied, he submerges the pot into the hole and spreads the soil, much hard clay, around the top.

"That should keep it in place," he says, and I nod.

I stand a moment longer, walk across the road (path, really) to my husband's plot, and mine, and then return to the car. The wind has picked up, and my son backs up so that the headlights reveal the lone flower in our family plot, at the grave of my mother, who, in moments of melancholy, wondered who would come to visit her grave, who would leave flowers.

The Parmenter family plot is approximately eight feet wide by thirty feet long and contains the graves of my great-grandmother, a great-aunt and great-uncle, an infant cousin, my grandmother, grandfather, mother, aunt, and uncle. My other aunt is buried a short distance away in a family plot with her husband and their children. My husband's parents, who relocated to be near us from their farm seventy miles away, are in their own plot a little farther to the east. Of these many family graves, very few contain the remains of individuals who were born in this town. Yet they came here and made a life here. My mother was born and died here, having never left the town. My sister was born here but died in Minnesota, where she was living with a son and his family. She was cremated, but her remains are not here. A cemetery, or graveyard, as we used to say, has many stories to tell, both in the absence and presence of graves and in where they are located, about family relations and connections.

Why, for example, do some people stay in one place and others move? What does it mean to root one's self, to plant oneself, as firmly as my son hoped to plant that poinsettia, in a community? What does a lifetime commitment to a hometown entail and reveal about the individual?

Christmas morning, we awake to snowflakes whirling and dancing about. In no time at all, snow covers the ground. We are busy preparing Christmas dinner for my nephew, who is driving over from a nearby town to spend the day with us. We do not drive up to the cemetery to see the lone spot of red and green in our family plot. We leave the poinsettia in the snow.

❄ ❄ ❄

Where do we come from? How do we get where we are? Why do we choose either to stay or move on? My uncle spent many years conducting genealogical research, with which he began to answer questions that his father, my grandfather, had about his ancestors. In particular, my mother's father wanted to know more information about his father, who had died when my grandfather was but a boy. The answers took my uncle to a variety of places, tracing back the family name, "Parmenter," beyond the family's arrival to America in the Revolutionary Period to fifteenth-century France. Actually, my uncle liked to claim that the Parmenter name emerged from the ancient Greek philosopher Parmenides, and who knows. Less sketchy records exist for Antoine-Augustine Parmentier, who made a case for the potato, previously considered inedible, to France during the reign of Louis XVI. Parmentier demonstrated his marketing skills by presenting a bouquet of potato blossoms to the king on his birthday, blossoms that Marie Antoinette and the ladies of the court then wore in their hair. Fame and fortune had not been so kind to all the Parmenters in France. Many who were Protestant Huguenots had been forced in previous generations to escape Catholic France for England. Ultimately, they would make the voyage to America, settling initially in New England.

My maternal grandmother's family, the Broiles, emerged from French lineage as well. The earliest arrivals from France were Thomas and Susannah January (Janvier) whose son Peter (Pierre Janvier) was born in Philadelphia in 1725. Both he and his four sons fought in the Revolutionary War before relocating in 1780 from Pennsylvania to Kentucky with other settlers on large flat boats, down the Ohio River. Warfare with Native Americans was still an ever-present threat, so upon their arrival the family stayed at a fort (Spring Station) near Louisville for a period of time before moving to the fort at Harrodsburg, Kentucky, and finally the fort at Lexington, which the males of the January family helped construct (or reconstruct). Ultimately, Peter January's son, Ephraim, who had been awarded one thousand acres of "bounty" land from the federal government for his participation in the Revolutionary War, settled southwest of Lexington in what would become Jessamine County. Ephraim later donated an acre of land for a cemetery and the first church (Ebenezer, a Presbyterian congregation), where many of the settler families would worship and later be buried, including Peter and Deborah January, his parents, as well as Ephraim and his wife, Sarah McConnell January. Our branch of the January family, a son of Ephraim's, Robert Wilson, who became a doctor, would relocate with his wife, Harriet (Postlethwaite), to Tennessee after the birth of their daughter, Mary Eliza January, in Logan County, Kentucky. From there the trail of names, appearing and reappearing in later generations of family members, winds its way ultimately to Texas. Mary Eliza would marry Andrew G. Price of Richmond, and the two settled in Christiana, Tennessee. Their daughter, Hattie Ellen Price, would marry Francis T. Broiles of Hoover Gap, Tennessee, and the couple would have nine children, of which my grandmother, Mary Sue Broiles, was the second oldest. After the death of their mother, Hattie Ellen, the Broiles children moved with their father, Francis, to Clarksville and later Lindsey, south of Bonham, in east Texas. There my grandmother, Mary Sue Broiles, already grown, would meet and marry my grandfather, William E. Parmenter. Rather than hailing from Kentucky and Tennessee, W. E.'s father had moved from the state of New York to the Midwest, the area around Jacksonville, Illinois, where he and Mary Elizabeth Buchanan met and married. And that is where my uncle ventured in the 1970s in order to reunite, in one sense, our family.

In 1948 I accompanied my mother and grandfather to Illinois, between Springfield and Jacksonville, to visit the area where my great-grandfather had lived and died. With the help of a cousin who lived near Springfield, we received directions to a small farm east of Jacksonville where we found a few gravestones in the middle of a pasture. There stood a columnar gravestone marking the site of my great-grandfather's grave. The visit settled my grandfather's mind, who provided money to have a fence built to enclose the graves, but my uncle decided a few decades later to request permission to move the gravestone, but not exhume the remains of the deceased, from the country cemetery in Illinois to our family plot in the cemetery in my hometown of Throckmorton, Texas. Permission received, my uncle had the stone shipped and positioned in the family plot, alongside the graves of my grandfather's mother; his sister, Mary Alice (Henson); and my grandfather, rejoining father, wife, (one) daughter, and son, at least epigraphically.

While it is no doubt important how my family got to America, my grandfather told me firsthand how he arrived in Texas. W. E. (William Eugene) Parmenter was born on September 25, 1858, in a little log cabin eight miles east of Jacksonville, Illinois. The little log house had one big room and one side room. He was the child of Mary Elizabeth Buchanan, born March 26, 1837, and Calvin Eugene Parmenter, born February 14, 1833. His father, Calvin Eugene, moved from New York state to Illinois, where he met and married Mary Elizabeth Buchanan in 1855. W. E. Parmenter was the eldest of three, having two younger sisters. The older sister, Mary Alice Parmenter, was born November 24, 1860, and the younger sister, Ellen Roxana Parmenter, was born April 21, 1863. The following year tragedy met the family when the children's father, Calvin Eugene, died on August 18, 1864, at the age of thirty-one, from complications related to a gunshot wound. He had attended a rally in nearby Springfield and was returning to his home near Jacksonville on a flat rail car when he was accidentally shot, presumably by the firearm of someone else in attendance. His twenty-seven-year-old widow, Elizabeth, now had three children to rear, the oldest, W. E., only six years old. My grandfather, having lost his father when he was but a child, had few memories, but one was particularly strong. On a visit to Springfield, Illinois, with his father, a very young W. E. saw many saloons and many drunken soldiers. He asked his father what was the matter with all the men, and his father answered, "Son, the men are drunk." The image and remark by his father stayed in his memory, and W. E. rarely touched alcohol.

Not too long after her husband's death, W. E.'s mother bought a thirty-acre farm. My grandfather made a crop of corn in the spring after he turned eleven years old. In the wintertime snow would stack up a foot deep, and W. E. would have to kick it back for the girls as they walked three miles to school.

In 1871 the family sold the farm and moved to a small town between Jacksonville, Illinois, and Quincy, Illinois, which was the second-largest city in the state at the time. They stayed there one winter, and in the spring of 1872 they left for Texas, with Elizabeth's brother-in-law and his children, taking a steamboat from Quincy, Illinois, sometime during the month of March. They traveled down the Mississippi and had to change vessels in St. Louis as their boat was too large to pass under the bridge. From there they traveled down to the mouth of the Red River where again they changed transportation, boarding an even smaller craft to traverse the Red River to Clarksville, Texas.

The boat from St. Louis to the mouth of the Red River was a double-decked boat, the bottom deck for freight and the upper deck for passengers. South of Natchez, Mississippi, across the river from Fort Adams was where they entered the Red River (called Avoyelles/Concordia on a Louisiana map). The ports of call on the Red River today are Alexandria, Natchitoches, Coushatta, and Shreveport. In the nineteenth century, however, before the arrival of the trains, the banks of the Red River were dotted all along the way with docks and warehouses and citizens in the communities along them who eagerly awaited the steamships for their transportation and transport needs.

Somewhere near Caspiana (Caddo Parish, Louisiana) the boat had drifted off-river into what W. E. called the Black Bayou and could hardly hold its own passengers and freight. As he recalled, the African-Americans had to tie ropes on the boat and get on skiffs to try to tow the craft to deeper water. They tied the ropes on the wrong side, and the skiffs turned over. Three men got on another skiff to help them, and, with the combined efforts of all, they drifted back out into the Red River. They saw a deer out in the water, and they floated by and roped it. Then they took their knives and cut its throat. It was the first venison my grandfather had ever tasted.

In traveling to Texas by steamship my grandfather and his family experienced a form of transportation on its way out of existence. Before the arrival of railroads to Texas in the 1860s, steamships provided the primary means of transporting goods and people to and from a state that also involved an overland route getting to or from a river landing or port. In the south of Texas that port was Galveston; in the east it was Jefferson, situated on the Big Cypress and separated from the Red River by Lake Caddo; and in north Texas it was Clarksville, fifteen miles south of Rowland's Landing, a port on the Red River between Texas and Oklahoma. Clarksville and Jefferson were served by steamships plying the Red River from the Mississippi across Louisiana, transporting goods, including cotton, and immigrants to Texas, a sovereign republic as of 1836 and a state of the US as of 1845. In fact, as Charles Shirley Potts reports in his history of the railroads of Texas, at a time when Dallas and other cities did not exist and before the railroads arrived, Jefferson served as the trading center of east and north Texas, only trailing Galveston in its amount of freight. Likewise, Clarksville, founded in 1835, commanded most of the trade in north Texas, reportedly sending freight out overland to points as far west as El

Paso. But with the construction in the 1870s of the Texas Central from Houston to Dallas and the Texas & Pacific extending to Shreveport and the Transcontinental branch providing access to St. Louis via Texarkana, the railroads effectively took control of passenger and freight transportation.

My grandfather and his family left the steamboat about sixteen miles north of Clarksville, Texas, at Rowland's Landing and hired a man to take them (by wagon and oxen) to Clarksville. There they met up with another man going to the community of Lindsey (now Randolph, southwest of Bonham) where they wanted to go, so they accompanied him on the eighty-mile journey on his wagon with two yoke of oxen. As it was springtime, the family gathered wild strawberries all across Lamar County. Arriving around the middle of April, the family knew it was too late to put in a crop, so they bought land and built a house. My grandfather worked that summer for Jim Buchanan for fifty cents a day and dinner. His sisters caught the measles on the steamship, and his sister Ellen had a relapse after arriving in Bonham. She died on June 24, 1872, and is buried in a family graveyard (Buchanan, about ten miles southwest of Bonham, called the Lindsey community, now called Randolph, Texas).

When he was eighteen years old, my grandfather hired out to drive cattle from Leonard pens to Mud Creek about 125 miles away, which took five or six days to make the trip. Although there were no Indian sightings, it proved to be a very interesting trip, introducing him to new parts of the countryside.

W. E. married Eller "Ella" Blackburn on November 29, 1882, near Bonham and rented land to farm. Mozella was born November 12, 1883, and Sudie Roxana was born May 21, 1887. Mozella, or Aunt Dale as we called her, married Charlie Trotter, and the youngest of their children, my cousin Heloise (Baker), at ninety, still lives out west in Wellman, Texas.

While W. E. and Ella were living near Bonham, an infamous crime took place. Eli and Sam Dyers, horse and cattle thieves who had forfeited their bond, returned to Bonham to hide out. When the local sheriff, Tom Ragsdale, heard of their presence, he rounded up a small posse to capture them. In the midst of their escape the Dyers brothers killed both Sheriff Ragsdale and a member of his posse (Joe Buchanan). After they were captured and held in jail, they were mobbed by the people of the surrounding communities (about five hundred) and hanged from a bois d'arc tree. In May 1885 my grandfather witnessed the events leading up to this, the anger of the community, and the public hanging.

Meanwhile, his wife, Ella Blackburn Parmenter, developed tuberculosis, and so in the fall of 1889 he traveled with her to a more favorable climate for her health. They spent the fall of 1889 in Abilene and from there traveled to Kerrville in the spring. At the age of twenty-nine, Ella died on March 20, 1891. W. E. had to sell his wagon and team and take his wife's body back to Bonham on the train.

After Ella's burial, he stayed in the Lindsey community. On August 21, 1892, he met Mary Sue Broiles, and on October 27, 1892, married her. They lived in Bonham and farmed for a few years. Here Calvin Wayne Parmenter was born on August 25, 1893, and that fall they moved to Cooke County. My uncle liked to joke that he and his mother were *pioneers*: she was pioneering motherhood and he was, of course, pioneering babyhood. In Cooke County the family lived and farmed and on April 14, 1896, welcomed the birth of a daughter, Hattie Elizabeth. On the move, the family relocated to Indian Territory (Oklahoma) in the fall of 1897 to farm and trade. There my grandfather had a fine span of mules stolen on the night of October 31, 1889. In December 1901 they moved to Throckmorton County, Texas, because he wanted to go west and also because his sister, (Mary) Alice Henson, now married, lived in Throckmorton County. Rena Mae, my mother, was born on January 9, 1902, on a cold, snowy night in a two-room house that the family had bought. It was a new house but built open, so they had to put a tarp over Mary Sue, my grandmother, to keep the snow off of her and her newborn baby, Rena. Dr. J. E. Harrell, the first man they met in Throckmorton, was the attending physician. That doctor would deliver my sister in the same house twenty-two years later and then be present at my birth as well two years later. Mother and both daughters were born in the same house and delivered by the same doctor. My mother and her husband lived with her parents at the time and helped with the farming of the many acres. When my sister was five years old, my grandfather bought a house in town, one block from the school, so my sister and I would not have to walk the five miles to the Bush Knob Community School or ride the bus to the school in Throckmorton each day.

After moving to Throckmorton, W. E. bought a 320-acre farm and gradually purchased additional acreage until he owned 1,500 acres total. W. E. was tax assessor from 1904 to 1908 (two terms). During World War I, he served as county agent in 1918 for a term until the younger men returned from war. From 1901 until his death in 1951 my grandfather farmed and ranched in Throckmorton. Initially the family lived in a two-room house that was on the home place. Grandfather added three more rooms to the house, and the family lived there until 1928, when they purchased a home in town. Like many farmers of the day, Grandfather rotated the crops he planted in the fields: cotton one year, maize the next, wheat, oats, and barley on other years. The cotton was taken to the local gin for processing. Even as young girls my older sister and I were taken to the fields to help Mother and Grandfather chop weeds out of the cotton rows. Local farmhands would be hired for pulling the cotton. Machinery was brought in to "head" or chop off the heads of the maize, which was then kept for feed for the livestock (cows, horses, etc.). Although combines are used in wheat fields today, Grandfather would often bring in a steam-operated threshing machine to separate the kernels of the wheat, oats, or barley from the stalk. The wheat was taken to the local elevator, where it was purchased by the bushel and shipped into Fort Worth. A small portion of the wheat Grandfather would take to a mill at Stamford to be processed into flour for use by our family. The oats and barley served as feed for the cattle, hogs, and chickens. The remainder stalks from these fields would be cut with a binder and gathered into stacks for hay. My grandfather did his own planting, and my mother was his plow-hand. She and Grandfather would leave early for the farm to harness the team of horses to the plows, each plow having two horses. From sunup to noon Mother and Grandfather would plow, stopping for lunch and continuing to sunset. A given field might take several days to complete, and the jerking of the plow as the horses dragged it through the rocky land left bruises on my mother's arms and legs. On years during drought conditions when the stock pond or "tank" was low, my mother would hitch up the team to a "scraper" and dredge the muck from the bottom of the pond. According to a slip of paper my grandfather left to instruct my mother on planting season, and the need to have the land plowed and ready, wheat was to be planted between the middle of October to the middle of November. Little black wheat was to be planted around the first of December. Oats were to be sown by the middle of January. Corn was to be sown during the period of the dark moon, right after the full moon, in February. Maize was to be planted in March in the period of the dark moon, after the full moon. Cotton was to be planted on the first or twentieth of May. In addition to caring for the fields, there were barbed wire fences that needed attention, lest cactus or mesquite trees grow up along the fence line and pull down wires and posts, letting out cattle. Grandfather kept a herd of Hereford cattle, numbering anywhere from thirty to one hundred, depending on the year and which land he had leased. When it came time to work the cattle, he hired some men to help round up and brand the animals. His ranch brand was the diamond, and the few cattle owned by my mother had the diamond brand with a bar underneath it. Calves born of these cattle were taken to sale, and one had to be vigilant in protecting both cow, calf, and herd from packs of coyotes. As a child I would ride to the farm in the pickup with my grandfather and climb on the roof when he stopped in order to help him get an accurate count of the herd. One of my grandfather's great-granddaughters recently has applied to the State of Texas for recognition of the family having owned and farmed the land for one hundred years or more.

For as long as I can remember, the First National Bank of Throckmorton has printed an image of the head of a Hereford cow along with a slogan in italics: *Throckmorton, Capitol of Cow Country*. In fact, as Walter Merriman, longtime historian of Throckmorton County, reports, Lee Atkinson, president of the Chamber of Commerce and the local Rodeo Association, coined the slogan in 1936 as a way to compete with surrounding towns that had their own slogans, such as Albany's "Home of the Hereford." And, in fact, the slogan is accurate: ranching, farming, and, later, oil production represent the main business in my hometown. As John Leffler reports about Throckmorton at the Texas State Historical Association website, corn was the crop most often planted in the late nineteenth century, and at nine hundred acres, not so much of that. Livestock, on the other hand, numbered high, with thirty-two thousand cattle and seven thousand sheep, with the number of head of cattle growing to forty-seven thousand by the turn of the century, as well as cultivated land, which stood at eight thousand acres (five thousand in cotton, increasing to twenty-one thousand acres by 1910; three thousand in corn). Farms and ranches, of various sizes, varying in number from five to six hundred, approximately half owned by local families, the other half rented, constitute the landscape, with wheat (today more often than cotton) representing a primary crop. Hereford, Charlois, Angus, Red Angus, Simmental, and Hotlander (a composite breed developed on the R. A. Brown Ranch) are the primary breeds of cattle to be found. While most of my extended family did not continue the farming and ranching occupation of my grandfather, some other larger operations have, notably the R. A. Brown Cattle Company and the (Ross) McKnight Ranches. Other early farming and ranching families included the Wrights, Allens, Davises, and Daws.

But what was Throckmorton before these early pioneer families? It was prairie, home to nomadic Native Americans, big bluestem and little bluestem grasses waving in the wind. And to cactus. Although many people associate the prickly pear cactus with west Texas, I always think of the fishhook cactus. Also known as the "pincushion" cactus because of its round shape, it is low to the ground with interwoven needles. Its importance, from my perspective, however, is the fruit it yields: small, red, elongated, one-half inch to two inches, in the shape of a small red pepper. The fruit extends from the fishhook cactus base sufficiently to ensure safe picking and eating. While not all cactus fruits are edible, these "cactus berries," as we called them, certainly are and provided a kind of Easter egg hunt excursion for me and my cousins as a child. I remember Mother taking her mother, me, and my sister, Musetta, to visit our Aunt Hattie and Uncle "D" (Louis David) Lilly out at their farm toward Woodson. It must have been in March around the time of my cousin John William's birthday because Aunt Hattie sent my sister and our cousins, Francis (Frank) and Madeline, with John William in charge, to gather "cactus berries" so she could make John William a birthday pie. Of course we ate the fresh fruit along the way but managed to return with enough for the dessert, which by comparison, when cooked into a syrupy pie, was a bit slick and slimy. I preferred the fresh fruit, sweet and tart. One needs a sharp eye to find these berries, what with competition from birds and other creatures, since one usually finds only five or six to a plant.

Many of these cacti were, no doubt, introduced to the north-central part of Texas in the way that mesquite trees were, by happenstance rather than plan. And like the many hardy species of cactus, the mesquite tree can survive dry conditions, even droughts it would seem, and other extreme forms of weather, heat or cold. During some of the driest times in Throckmorton, during the 1930s, some ranchers gathered mesquite beans in pods from the trees to feed cattle. Certainly it was not the best feed, as I remember one milk cow to which we fed the mesquite beans returned the favor by producing milk with a noticeably different flavor and even slightly tinged color, or so it seemed to me. How grateful we were for rains that provided both humans and animals with crops to consume.

The town and county of Throckmorton were dry then, as now: approximately nine hundred square miles of land with three square miles of water and a total average rainfall of only twenty-five inches. Only a small portion of the Brazos River flows through the county, the Salt Fork of the Brazos through the northeast corner and the Clear Fork through the southern; streams include Elm Creek and King Creek, which feed into lakes, Paint Creek, Millers Creek, Hog Creek, Boggy Creek, Lambs Head, and Walnut Creek, and which represent some other water sources winding their way across the county. It is not pleasant-tasting water, mineral and saline rich, prompting many to blend it with caffeinated tea, perhaps with a little sugar, for the cowboy cocktail of "iced tea," rather than drink it straight. But that is water from Lake Throckmorton, a reservoir constructed in 1918 and enlarged in 1940, on the city water system. There are folks in the country, obtaining their water from a tank or stock pond, which after a heavy rain stirs up sediment, who are presented with a muddy glass of water from the faucet. Or the water might come from a cistern, filled by water from the heavens and stored underground in a brick- or rock-lined hole, or from a well, dug deep; but the flavor of the water is informed by the distinctive soil of the county. Such a paucity of water means that many minerals have not been leached out of the soil of the county, much of it limestone or shale and rocky. Water, in whatever its form, is precious and not to be wasted. In those years of drought ranchers have filled trailer tanks with such precious water to haul it to town to share with residents, whose parched planted trees would have died without it. Planting a tree, digging a grave, digging anything is no easy task; rock, clay, soil hardened and dried deep by the sun is not easily extracted. In earlier times horses struggled to pull plows, straining at this dry earth. One-way disc plows often scraped only the surface, contributing in other parts of the Plains to the challenges of the Dust Bowl. It is a tough and demanding land that punishes as often as it rewards the hard efforts of its tenants. A good wheat crop, given the year, might be only fifteen to twenty bushels to the acre. These fields differ from the nutrient-rich lands to the north, Nebraska, Iowa, and other states that benefitted from an ancient glacial cover, contemporary fertilization and irrigation practices, drawing on rivers and the great underground water source of the Ogallala Aquifer, and that yield eighty to one hundred bushels of corn, seemingly unimaginable in my region. This, of course, is not to say that these other regions do not face their own challenges—blight, drought, hail, tornadoes are a part of life there as well. But the land, what we start out with, differs in incredibly significant ways, and surely must inform different regional perspectives and expectations of the norm.

My hometown is no Currier and Ives print that we found painted on plates in a store. It was not a Norman Rockwell village in the Berkshires of Massachusetts. No horse-drawn sleigh pulls up through the snow to the village green loaded with happy revelers bundled under a blanket. Or, to pick another season, no perfectly manicured pastures lead down to a bubbling brook of sparkling blue water where a group of boys frolic, having played hooky from school. No perfect haystacks stand in symmetrical order, pumpkins piled in a triumphant pyramid, multicolored leaves falling, kaleidoscopically, in an autumn breeze. This is not to say there is no beauty in my hometown, a tiny farming and ranching community in north-central Texas, no fun to be had by its residents or wayward schoolboys. Rather, it is to acknowledge a very different landscape, in which a winter snowfall, when it happens, is often preceded by a coating of treacherous ice; in which bales, now giant rolls of hay, are often scattered haphazardly through a field until needed or lined up sentinel-like to provide a windbreak for cattle unaccustomed to extended periods of harsh winter weather; in which trees, like mesquite and hackberry, do not yield colorful leaves—even those trees, such as fruitless mulberry, planted for their endurance in the unfriendly soil, merely show the change of season by yellowing leaves that persist in clinging to the branches until a winter freeze finally forces them to drop in an unhappy pile that is most often mulched; in which the few trees from afar, a maple, a blue spruce, stand out so strangely, in such glory, like a Yankee dialect heard in the coffee shop, that citizens marvel in their presence; in which pastures of prairie grass, some yellowed and dead from harsh summer sun and a lack of rain, are riddled with stickers and thorns of various kinds, including grass burrs and cactus, and predators to avoid, such as chiggers, red ant hills, and, of course, rattlesnakes.

Not a very lovely picture, one might say. But look to the sky as well, a sky that stretches across the horizon and changes colors for a magnificent sunset or dramatically for an approaching thunderstorm from the west, from as far away as the mountains of New Mexico, or for a blue norther line extending across the northwest skies, moving steadily, ominously closer, dropping the temperature twenty, thirty, forty degrees, seemingly in a matter of minutes, as the front blows in, from Colorado, Montana, Canada, wherever the last barbed wire to the north was let down, or snapped, as the ranchers might joke, letting in the cold. Saddle a horse, ride out to the edge of town, or into the countryside, look below the horizon at the sparse landscape: pick out a lone tree; identify a distant landmark; note a butte or a knob with trees, or rather, bushes on it, which provided the name for a small community near where I was born called Bush Knob. Check the creek where the boys might play hooky: is there enough water for swimming, for wading? Is its color reddish as the sand of the Salt and Clear forks of the Brazos rivers, both of which run through the county? Do you detect fossils in the embankment? Flintstones that once served as arrow tips within a Native American's quiver? Can you distinguish among the prairie grasses big bluestem and little bluestem? Examine the diamond pattern in a discarded rattlesnake's skin; pack away a discarded rattle from that deadly snake. Are there cactus berries to be found?

History reports a Spanish explorer (Pedro Vial) traveling through the area in 1786, en route from San Antonio to Santa Fe. No written reports of this land, then, until the mid-1800s when a US military expedition passes through.

Established in 1858 out of the earlier Fannin County (1837) in the Republic of Texas, Throckmorton was named for Dr. William E. Throckmorton, an early citizen of northern Texas, whose son, James Webb Throckmorton, served as state governor (1866) and congressman. Although established in 1858 with a town called Williamsburg, named in honor of Dr. Throckmorton, as its county seat, Throckmorton County was officially organized in 1879 with the town of Throckmorton as its new county seat. Foundation stones for the community of Williamsburg, located six miles north by slightly northwest of Throckmorton, can still be seen on McKnight ranch land.

Before it was a county, part of the land that makes up Throckmorton was home to a Comanche Indian Reservation for a short period of time in the mid-1850s. Camp Cooper, established to protect the reservation, was commandeered by the soon-to-be-famous Captain Robert E. Lee. Only a few years later, those living on the reservation were relocated to Oklahoma Indian Territory before the Civil War began. After the Civil War, Fort Griffin was established on the Clear Fork of the Brazos River just south of the Throckmorton County line in Shackelford County.

Hunting has always been an important part of the life of the county, with wild game in abundance. One particular form of hunting involved, curiously enough, coyotes and greyhounds. From some of the earliest days in the county, settlers brought in greyhound dogs to help with the capture and killing of coyotes, which, of course, threatened livestock. The popularity of these hounds in the hunts resulted in Throckmorton adopting the animal as its school mascot. According to Walter Merriman, author of a history of Throckmorton, the issue was seemingly settled with a comment made by Claude "Fuzz" Messenger. Fuzz was a member of the

1926 Throckmorton High School basketball team that made it to the state championship competition. Early in the century there were no divisions between small and large schools, and in the regional play-offs Throckmorton was pitted against the team of a city to the north, Wichita Falls High School, whose mascot was the Coyotes. Fuzz opined that surely even a large pack of coyotes from Wichita Falls could be caught and defeated by a few greyhounds. "So we'll be the Greyhounds." And so they were and defeated the Wichita Falls Coyotes. Even though Throckmorton did not win the state championship, they acquired a mascot, the sleek and fearless greyhound.

Curiously, today one does not often see greyhounds in Throckmorton. The hunting of coyotes by greyhounds seems to have ended. Coyotes, on the other hand, continue to thrive. Riding north toward Olney recently, I caught sight, through early morning mist, of three coyote pups as they raced across the highway and under a barbed wire fence, frolicking as young animals will do. And, for a while, another trio, or perhaps it was a quartet of coyotes—they must have been pups—passed near the backyard of my home, pausing to sing their mournful song on a number of successive evenings. One of my rancher neighbors heard that song too, I expect, and before the week was out, they sang no more. And truly, "the coyotes [that] wail along the trail" are primarily carnivores nonetheless, searching for a meal that often is a livelihood of a human. Whether by greyhound or shotgun, they become prey because of the prey they seek out.

✳ ✳ ✳

How many people do you know from small towns who joke that you must watch closely as you drive through their small town? As they say, "If you blink, you will miss it." Although only one blinking stoplight controls traffic where two highways, one north/south, the other east/west, meet, the geographical boundaries of the town of Throckmorton, at 1.7 square miles, allowing a passer-through to blink at least four or five times without missing it. Where the highways meet, the courthouse square sits on the northwest corner. Main Street, Minter Avenue, runs north and south, with the main commercial district running two blocks north. Drive far enough north and you will pass the clinic and hospital before meeting a fork in the highway that sends you to Seymour if you veer left, Olney if you veer right. Drive south and you will pass the city swimming pool and an RV/trailer park for hunters before climbing an escarpment on a highway that bounces along, roller coaster-like, toward Fort Griffin and Albany. Throckmorton County is a drainage basin for the Brazos River. Topographically, the town of Throckmorton sits at an elevation of approximately 1,200 to 1,300 feet above sea level with buttes rising to the south of town and ridges rising to the west and northwest of downtown, where the local schools perch at the top of a hill.

In terms of population, the town of Throckmorton has never been large, will probably never be large. At the turn of the twentieth century there were only 124 residents (1890). The population grew in the early twentieth century but even by the 1930 census the total population was 1,135. By mid-century Throckmorton had reached its peak with 1,319 residents, which declined to 1,105 in 1970, 1,036 in 1990, 905 in 2000, and 828 as of 2010. Yet this decline in population is not my story, or ultimately, probably the story of Throckmorton. Rather, it speaks to urbanization and migratory processes of people looking for employment. Those of us who stay behind have adapted as well, shopping at the one grocery store in town where once there were several and traveling to larger towns in the distance to buy cars and clothes and other products no longer available in our small town. Yet we persist with three cafés and a public library housed in the old train depot and churches and rodeo grounds and the school and community events that hold us together in what is, by birth or adoption, our hometown.

CHAPTER TWO

Growing Up, Putting Down Roots

O NE of the great events of my childhood was the arrival of the
train to Throckmorton on May 4, 1928. Texas & Pacific Railroad
built a spur (the "Cisco and Northeastern") from Cisco, which occupied
two lines, the Texas Central from near Waco to Rotan, just past Stamford, and, of course, the Texas & Pacific line that went from Fort Worth
west to Abilene and, ultimately, El Paso. In 1920 the T&P spur line had
been extended north from Cisco to Breckenridge. By 1927 construction
was underway to take the line thirty-seven miles north to Woodson with
Throckmorton as its terminus. The absolute end of the line was at the
stock pens, the site of the present-day annual livestock show, providing
ranchers a convenient means of transporting their cattle to sales in Fort
Worth. On the day the train arrived, at least ten thousand people crowded into Throckmorton to watch its arrival. Red, white, and blue bunting
adorned every building. Local and state politicians took the opportunity to make speeches. Cowboys and ranchers on horseback ushered the
train into town, one (Frank Rhoades, father of my future classmate Glow
Rhoades) had the plan of lassoing the smokestack and bringing the iron
horse to a halt. Indians came and staged a hunt, with buffalo that had been
brought in for the special occasion. A recently constructed depot, which
today serves as the community library, was sparkling new and ready for
travelers. Mother took my sister and me down for the event. Just recovered

from whooping cough, we grew warm in the swelling crowd and before long began coughing. Mother received a number of dark looks from others in the crowd for bringing us out, but who wanted to miss the arrival of the train? Although I was only three years old, I would have occasion to ride the train, as it would continue its service to Throckmorton until 1942 when the line was closed. In the mid-1930s when I was old enough to travel, my sister, older cousin, younger cousin, and I took the train down to Woodson to see my uncle, the Methodist minister, and his wife.

Were we excited as the locomotive, passenger, and freight cars pulled out of town and began rumbling along the tracks, built with care by men and mule teams, through prairie, dotted with mesquite trees and cactus. Each time the train would hit a rough spot in the tracks, my younger cousin Francis would call out loudly, "Oops, had a blowout," much to our embarrassment. The conductor would respond, "No, it is not a blowout. We do not have rubber tires on this train."

While the arrival of the train caused a great deal of commotion, daily life, as I recall it, was a bit simpler. Many Saturdays of my childhood were spent at the Texan Theatre, owned and operated by Mr. W. D. (Dub) Howsley, a dairy farmer who lived northeast of town on the highway to Olney. The first "picture show," operated by A. L. (Bud) Thompson, is reported to have been on South Minter Avenue at the site of the former Chevrolet dealership. After it burned to the ground in 1919, the result of a fire connected with the projection equipment, Mr. Howsley opened the Queen Theater, across and up the street a bit, near the former location of Scarlett Butane. My mother recalled attending silent movies in these theaters during her teenage years, around the time of World War I. In 1927 Mr. Howsley built a new building, two doors north of the bank, and opened the new Texan Theatre. My mother allowed me to attend the movie, often with my sister, on Saturday afternoons and received a complete summary of the experience when I would return home. She used to joke that she would give me a dime to go to the movies and a dime when I returned home in order to finish my summary quickly and be quiet. I enjoyed the serial Westerns on Saturday afternoons, so much so that I once stayed to watch the show again. My grandfather was waiting for me at the Masonic Hall just up the street and paddled me all the way home, it seemed. I begged him for us not to pass by the Methodist preacher's home because I did not want Brother Hand to see me being punished by another hand.

While Grandfather was the mayor of Throckmorton, Mr. Howsley would give him two free passes for a movie each year, so my mother could attend on occasion, when someone was able to sit with her mother, who was often bedfast with asthma and a heart condition. For a promotional event connected with the release of one of Shirley Temple's movies in 1932, Mr. Howsley featured a Shirley Temple doll and then drew from the ticket numbers to give the doll away. Mine was not the lucky ticket (I never have been lucky with chances!); a young bachelor from Woodson, Jewel Ridley, won the doll. I wept all the way out of the theater. Mr. Ridley, observing my distress, asked my mother what price she would give for the doll. My mother said she did not know, but it could not be much—indeed, it could not; we were all of us firmly in the jaws of the Great Depression.

"What would you take for the doll?" my mother asked.

"How about seven dollars?" he asked.

My mother looked at me, looked at the doll, and nodded. She wrote a check and Shirley was mine, for Christmas and for birthday. I still have the doll. For many years Shirley resided in my cedar chest, and when I found her in the 1980s, she was a bit the worse for wear. I took her to Abilene to be restrung and rewigged, while I made her a new red-and-white polka dot dress. She then took up residence in an elementary school desk that we bought when the old school building was demolished. Whenever I am in the guest bedroom, she sometimes gives me a look as though she would like to stop studying at that desk, get up, and dance for a while. But at our respective ages, we have to take it a bit easy.

In 1940 Mr. Howsley sold the theater and a couple of different owners operated it before selling it to a young man who had just completed a tour of duty in the army. Thus, in 1946, Mr. J. B. and Mrs. Inez Thompson, parents of my future student and attorney Bill and his sister Nancy Jane, began operating the theater. With a center and two side aisles and an orchestra pit in front for the piano player during its silent movie days, the theater, with balcony, seated approximately four hundred. The Thompsons updated the theater, adding a glassed-in cry room and new technical equipment, the former, Bill Thompson reports, used primarily by his family since all mothers with babies assured the Thompsons that their children would stop crying after a few minutes. Bill's father, J. B., also operated a theater in nearby Woodson and purchased the Royal Theater in Archer City (home of Larry McMurtry, author of *The Last Picture Show*) as well. The Thompsons operated the local theater until 1956 when television made running a movie theater no longer profitable in our small town.

For such a small town we had a thriving community. Other businesses included four grocery stores ("M" System Grocery and Market owned by Tom Morrison, Hugh L. Smith, Midway Grocery and Market, and Huston's Food Store; Mr. Huston's daughter, Marilyn, was a friend of mine); the Ideal Bakery; two drugstores (Hardy Drug and City Pharmacy); a jewelry store (owned by Kenneth Cowan, for whom I worked during Christmas holidays); two dry goods stores (Henry L. Smith and Hugh L. Smith—yet they were not related); a variety store (Mr. and Mrs. Ray Fry); a lumberyard (Morrison-Smith, operated by Mr. Roy Franks); a hardware and furniture store (owned by Ed Merriman, who would also open a funeral home); a doctor's office and dentist's office above the Midway Grocery Store (operated by Dr. Berry and Dr. Guice, respectively); a barbershop (operated by Mr. Jeff Burrows and Mr. Burt Lilly, the latter who seemed to delight in giving me shorter-than-necessary page-boy haircuts, before I was old enough for the beauty salon); a couple of beauty parlors (Cinderella Beauty Parlor owned by Mrs. H. S. Neely and another operated in her home by Mrs. Manuel and her daughter); two insurance and abstracting companies (owned by S. D. Liles and B. F. Reynolds); several cafés (one operated by Lank Milligan, when I was in high school, in the current location of Coalson's Grocery Store, and Skeet's Café, owned by Skeet Hethcock, across from the firehouse); a Chevrolet dealership located north of the Texan Theatre; a Ford dealership on a side street south of the stoplight on the main street (operated by Mr. Jim Merrill); and the First National Bank housing offices, including an attorney, and the telephone operator's headquarters just upstairs.

As the bank building was located halfway up the block of the main street, the telephone office on the second floor was centrally located. The telephone operator, Mrs. Blackshire, or her assistants, could look out the east- and south-facing windows up and down the main street, able to spot anyone who happened to be downtown that a caller might be seeking. When the staff of Midway Grocery (owned by Homer Redwine and later by Mr. Dawes and then Blaine Estridge) did not answer their telephone promptly enough, Mrs. Blackshire would raise her window and call out across the street to alert Midway Grocery that they needed to answer their phone, her voice evidently more effective than the jangling bells of the machine. Eunice (Mrs. Belton) Redwine served as one of Mrs. Blackshire's assistants and reported to my mother how much she enjoyed listening in on the line, in later years, when my sister and I would call from college. Evidently it was quite the conversation, with each of us grabbing the receiver from the other to share our news or finish the other sister's sentence. When my sister Musetta called to report the birth of her first son, many years later, the operator patched the call through not only to my mother but to the office where I was working as well. I miss that kind of local telephone service!

Having been born in 1925, I was less a jazz baby than a child of the Depression. In fact, my memories of childhood often involve how my family got by. We were fairly self-sufficient: we planted gardens, in town and at the farm, for black-eyed peas, English peas, corn, cucumbers, onions, and potatoes. We grew wheat, a portion of which we kept and had milled into fine flour at Stamford. We kept animals for produce. In town we had a cow that provided milk for our dairy needs of butter and clabber (a kind of sour yogurt or cottage cheese—in Germany they call it quark; in France, crème fraiche); the cream we would sell to a local distributor. We kept about a dozen chickens to provide eggs. Through the year we kept two hogs in town for slaughter during the first cold spell, often November. Grandfather would have a neighbor shoot the hogs through the head, and then he would skin the carcass and retrieve the various cuts of meat for preparation: the ham, bacon, and shoulder were packed in salt in a wooden box in the back of the car shed; other parts were ground and made into sausage, which were then stored in muslin sacks and hung in the rafters of the car shed. The fat of the hog was then cooked outside over an open fire in two large black iron pots (which I still have) through the day. At night we let the mixture cool; the lard would rise to the top and congeal. The next morning we would skim the lard from the top and store it in cans for future use. Utilizing the crackling of the hog meat, we would add water and lye to the black kettles and cook the mixture, stirring it through the day with a wooden paddle. The next day we would cut the congealed mixture, now lye soap, into squares and store it on planks in the car shed. We used this lye soap for washing dishes, clothes, and our hair.

What we could not produce or grow, we bought at the grocery store: body soap, salt, pepper, sugar, baking powder, soda, vanilla extract, coffee, and the like—most in bulk that were kept in the storm cellar. Thus, our two-year credit at Morrison Grocery during the mid-1930s totaled only eighty dollars. Because we did not have fruit trees in town or at the farm, we would purchase fruit (peaches, plums, apples, bananas, etc.) in bulk and consume what we could before canning the rest to store in the storm cellar where they would stay cool.

We also could not produce boots—red ones—and that is what my good friend Adrienne Smith had because her father, Hugh L., owned Smith Grocery and Dry Goods (currently the location of a restaurant, Between the Forks, owned by my former student Thomas Ash). I begged and begged my mother for a pair of these boots. Finally she relented, with my agreement that like the Shirley Temple doll from some years before, these boots would serve as both my Christmas and birthday gift for the year. I readily agreed. I so wanted those boots. And so I had them. And as they were my "shoes" for the year, I wore them everywhere: to school, to church, to town, anywhere I went. I cannot say, unlike Nancy Sinatra, that those "boots were made for walking." All I know is that the following year when it came time for a new pair of shoes, I did not ask for boots. I can also say that even as an adult, a sharp pair of shoes, or even boots, still catch my eye.

When it came time for eighth-grade graduation, Hugh L. Smith's wife, Bert (short for Roberta), provided the bolt of material so that each of us,

Adrienne, I, and our other good friend Dorothy Condron, could have an identical dress. Each of our mothers made a dress, and then Bert took us to Abilene to find pink-and-red sandals to match the material. I am sure that we Three Musketeers made quite the entrance into Rice Auditorium, but none of the administrators got us confused or our names wrong as they presented diplomas.

In the midst of the Depression, however, I had to learn lessons about limits and about waiting my turn. So I waited until my older sister completed her time in Pep Squad before I was able to join. Our Pep Squad had around thirty members in it who supported, and accompanied, the three cheerleaders to home and away football games, providing a "response" to the "call" of the cheerleaders' yells and chants. To be a member of the Pep Squad one needed the yellowish gold wool sweater and skirt—our school colors were purple and gold—that served as the uniform. One also needed to have spending money for a meal when attending away games. The school would send three buses: one for the football team, one for the band, and one for the cheerleaders and pep squad. I suppose that was when I really developed my vocal enthusiasm for football games, which I continued during my teaching years, then yelling for my student athletes rather than my classmates; today I still enjoy attending games to cheer our home team and faithfully follow the Dallas Cowboys as well.

✳ ✳ ✳

In recalling my teachers, I see a pattern that persisted for many years at the Throckmorton Schools: good teachers, some homegrown like me, some from elsewhere, came and stayed and watched generations of students pass through the halls, marveling at where the years had gone. Mr. Harry Rice, who was the school superintendent, received assistance from his brother, who worked in the placement center at North Texas State Teachers College in Denton, in filling vacant teaching positions at the school. Mr. Rice would hire young teachers, especially female, who were glad to get their start in teaching at Throckmorton and often found a husband among the ranks of young farmers and ranchers in the community.

As a kindergarten student I had Mrs. Cochran as a teacher, and later when I joined the faculty she was still teaching in the elementary school. At a meeting with teachers from a nearby school in the early 1950s, I encountered a young man (Bobby Boyd) I had taught in my first years at the school. He was now teaching at the nearby school of Woodson.

"Why, Bobby Boyd," I exclaimed. "I taught you and now here you are as a teacher. That makes me feel old."

Mrs. Cochran, standing nearby, smiled and said, "Yes, Minta, and I taught you in kindergarten, so imagine how old that makes me feel."

Mrs. Cochran, previously Lorene Bachman, a local girl, was a good teacher and the aunt of some future students of mine. She had been a first-grade teacher at Throckmorton in previous years before starting her family. So when she returned to teach, she was placed in kindergarten with seven pupils: one of them was I. The others were Glow Rhoades, Guy Rankin, Barbara K. Negy, Adrienne Smith, June Ball, and Wallace McDonald. The large first-grade class, however, had forty students. The class was split, and Mrs. Cochran's kindergarteners joined some of the first graders. Thus, I learned the first-grade curriculum, so my kindergarten year was also my first-grade year.

In the fall term of that first year, I watched as classmate after classmate celebrated his or her birthday and grew sadder as I realized that I would be waiting a long time for my March 31st birthday. By the middle of November I decided that enough was enough and that I, too, must have a fall birthday. So on November 14, at the end of the day, I announced to some of the girls in my class that it was my birthday and invited them home for my birthday party. My mother, surely surprised, did not say a word when I marched into the house with my line of guests trailing behind me, but quickly baked a hot milk cake and served us. When the girls left, I was made to understand, in the old-fashioned way, that I was not to lie, about birthdays or anything else, in the future. My grandfather, however, was delighted by my ingenuity, or nerve, or perhaps, like most grandparents, he recalled incidents with my mother from her childhood. In any case, for the rest of his life, he would provide birthday wishes, via a swat on my rump, every year on November 14.

As a result of learning the first-grade curriculum during my kindergarten year, I entered second grade a year early, with the wife of the doctor who brought me into the world, Mrs. J. E. Harrell, as my teacher. Kindly and older, she nurtured our class as Mrs. Cochran had done. Miss Dora Holt, my third-grade teacher, was a slim, single woman in her forties from Seymour, a town to the north, who wore severe dark-rimmed glasses and her dark hair in a bun. Despite her serious countenance, she was a good teacher and allowed me to enter the spelling bee; out of three hundred words, I missed one hundred and fifty. I have never been a good speller, which may explain why I excelled in talking rather than in writing, sometimes to excess. In fact, Miss Holt had occasion to reassure my mother about my talkative nature. "Don't worry about what Minta might tell at school about things that happen at home," she said. "All third graders tell everything they know in public." My talking out of turn was not so well received by my fourth-grade teacher, Mrs. Elizabeth McDonald, who spanked my hand with a ruler. In junior high school (grades six, seven, and eight), I had the same teachers for all three years: Miss Lera D. Irick (art), Miss Mary Sweet (English), Mrs. Peevey (math), and Mr. Heizer (history and principal). My classmates and I were happy to leave grouchy old Mrs. Peevey behind, or so we thought, when we entered high school. But just our luck, she followed us and became the high school math teacher. Certainly I did not chew gum in her high school math class, having had the side of my head powdered with chalk dust when Mrs. Peevey popped me with an eraser in junior high, having caught me chomping on gum.

I suppose I was a lively child, in word and deed. I loved baseball and would arrive at school early in order to join the other boys and girls in a game before classes began. I was always ready for an adventure. Occasionally my grandfather would take us to Breckenridge, if he had business, in a Buick we kept for at least a decade. Our shopping was mostly window-shopping, but it was fun nonetheless. Sometimes my mother allowed me to accompany Mrs. John ("Willie") Grable in her two-seated Ford car to Wichita Falls to sell eggs, stored carefully in her trunk, which she had purchased from farmers all over the county. It was a great lesson in learning how to be the middleman (or middle-woman, in this case) in business. For a really big trip, my mother paid my fare and allowed me to ride on the school bus to Dallas with Mrs. Grable, Billie John (her daughter), and other members of the community in 1936 to visit the exhibition grounds of the Texas Centennial celebration.

One of my trips as a youngster involved attending the Methodist Church camp at Buffalo Gap, south of Abilene. Because the local Methodist Church was two doors down from our family home, when something was happening at the church, my family was usually present. I was baptized as an infant (in August after my March birthday) at the Bush Knob Methodist Church. In Throckmorton, I joined the church as a child and so have been a member for well over seventy-five years. In those days, a perfect attendance pin was given to Sunday School members, and I received one, as much because of the ritual and good habits my mother and family instilled, I am certain, rather than my own good efforts. My family's persistence paid off and what started as routine became a part of me. All was not routine, however; there was fun to be had in connection with my developing faith. My mother, no doubt, thought that church camp would be a good holiday for me, and so it was. Two of the girls I met at camp would later be classmates of mine at the Methodist school I attended, McMurry College: Mary Ann Murray of Abilene and Betty Jo Barkley of Anson. At camp that year I also met Dallas Perkins, who would make a name for himself as an adult by creating a new community, Impact, to serve the alcohol needs of Abilene and surrounding areas. Dallas, who went into advertising, owned a small poultry farm north of Abilene, and recognizing that many men (and women) do not live by fowl alone, purchased some additional acreage adjacent to his property in order to create the village of Impact (named after his advertising business), a community that could legally sell alcohol. In 1960 he collected signatures of the residents to incorporate, and then later the residents voted to approve the sale of alcohol. The two liquor stores did a thriving business, bringing revenue to the community that allowed for paved streets, garbage collection, and other forms of community infrastructure. By 1978, however, the citizens of Abilene voted to legalize the sale of liquor, and Dallas's tiny community of Impact, with around fifty residents, became another suburb. For eighteen years, however, the thriving sales of the stores in Impact demonstrated Dallas's ingenuity both in sidestepping the strong moral sentiments about alcohol by many Abilene citizens, churches, and political leaders and in making a great deal of money while doing so. When the news about Impact hit the newspaper early in 1960, I followed the story with interest, once I knew it was led by someone I had met at church camp in Buffalo Gap so many years ago.

When travel opportunities did not present themselves during my growing up years, I found adventure at home or in the neighborhood—often adventures worth avoiding. Whenever my grandfather had not brought cattle into town and the milk cow was safely in her stall, friends or cousins would join me in jumping from the slanted roof of the barn into the lot behind our home. On one unhappy jump, I chipped a tooth in the process. Along with the milk cow, my grandfather always kept a horse in the lot on which he could ride out to the farm, if he wished. Whenever he and my mother took the Ford pickup, however, I might take advantage of the "transportation" left behind in order to pay my friends social calls. On one of these outings, I was returning from visiting my friend Sallie Lou Tharp, who lived near the school. Sallie Lou was a great deal of fun and quite talented too. She and a group of classmates (Jackie Rankin, Wanda Beth Taylor, G. B. McCarson, and Carroll Wade Pogue) formed a musical group known as Call of the Canyon, sponsored by Louise Russell Davis, the home economics teacher, and traveled to perform as far away as Fort Worth and as close to home as Pogue's Grocery Store. Whether it was a concert at Mineral Wells (Texas) at the Crazy Water Hotel or an intermission performance at a local rodeo, the Call of the Canyon always pleased the crowd with their trumpet, saxophone, and drum instrumentals and their vocal harmonies.

At any rate, after my visit to Sallie Lou, I mounted the horse where it had been tied in front of the Tharp house and headed for home. As I passed the tennis courts, a stray tennis ball hit the side of the horse, spooking it, and I took off on the ride of my life. The horse galloped down the street in front of the school; I had lost control of the reins and caught one of my feet in the stirrup. Holding onto the saddle horn, I called out for help as

I bounced along, biting my lip and ultimately my tongue, nearly in two, until I fell off the horse near home. Mr. Grable, a heart patient, who was sitting on his front porch, saw me and the horse sail by and my ill-timed fall. He scooped me up and carried me along the street until he was joined by Brother Hand, the Methodist minister, another heart patient, who grabbed hold and helped carry me up the back steps of my house where my mother had returned from the farm. She took one look at me and my bloody mouth and loaded me into the car to visit the doctor downtown. She was sufficiently worried so as not punish me for (a) taking the horse out without permission and (b) endangering the lives of two older men whose hearts needed no jump start by the antics of an injured girl thrown from a runaway horse. Downtown we went to Dr. Berry's office, above Midway Grocery, so that an expert could assess the damage. The front of my tongue was hanging loose; my lower lip was bleeding. No stitches were required after Dr. Berry applied the medicine, but he instructed me that I needed to keep my mouth shut. My mother, who had probably wished for this kind of silence all through my childhood, was eager, surprisingly enough, for me to begin speaking again when the weeks of silence had passed.

While my mother had her hands full dealing with me as a force of nature, there were other forces of nature with which she would not interact. I refer to tornadoes, to which my mother gave a full dose of respect. Although as far as I know she had never encountered a tornado in her younger years, as a parent with two daughters, she would jump into action at any sign of potentially violent weather. The storm cellar in our backyard, which preserved our canned fruit and other food supplies, was also my mother's refuge if she detected or suspected bad weather approaching. She would bundle my sister and me up and take us down to sleep in the cellar, furnished with a daybed, until the bad weather had passed. My grandfather refused to leave the house and my grandmother could not, so it was just my sister, my mother, and I in that underground cavern, waiting for whistling winds to subside.

Ultimately, the cellar would prove problematic; water would seep through the earthen walls and puddle in the floor. Finally Mother had it filled in and a new cellar dug in the early 1940s near the front porch of the house, this one with a cement floor and walls fitted with stone by Henry Boland, a mason, who had put the same talents to work for his home in the north part of town. She continued to watch the weather, and by the mid-1950s with the aid of television and the weatherman, Tom Crane and later Warren Silver and Ben Warren on Channel 3, the NBC affiliate in Wichita Falls, Texas, she persisted in shepherding not only my family into the cellar but her whole street of neighbors, many widows, who maintained a telephone chain during such weather, comparing notes and determining when to gather at the cellar. Such diligence would have made them excellent air raid wardens during World War II had Throckmorton, miles from anywhere, needed blackouts for safety from approaching Japanese or German aircraft.

When she would call about an approaching storm, I would gather my sons from their beds while my husband backed the car from the garage. We would drive over the hill to my mother's house where already we could see the shapes of little old ladies and others scurrying across yards or down the street to descend into the cellar. All, that is, except Mrs. Willie Shannon. Willie, who lived a distance away on the north highway near the hospital, would come careening down the road in her car as though Satan were at her heels, inevitably turning sharply to the left and sliding the car down a slight incline into the yard and screeching to a stop quite near the door of the cellar. Because of its size, the cellar hosted only women and children, unless the storm got particularly bad. The men would watch the sky from the covered wraparound front porch, talking about other storms, perhaps smoking a cigarette.

Ironically, the only tornado my mother really experienced was while sitting with my grandfather in the hospital in Olney in 1951, the year he died. The nurse had my mother help her set Grandfather up into a reclining chair and move him into the hall. There she sat and prayed as the storm howled about, destroying a good bit of the town but not the hospital. My mother's car had a two-by-four driven through one of the tires and another one driven through the front windshield through the rear window. We borrowed a knife from the hospital in order to cut the board out of the tire, change it, and drive the vehicle back to Throckmorton. While my mother and grandfather survived that storm, he did not leave the hospital, but died a week or so later at the age of ninety-three years.

But my childhood into adulthood trips to the storm cellar have swept us far away from my childhood, so like Dorothy in *The Wizard of Oz*, we will click our ruby slippers, or red cowboy boots, three times to return to my high school years.

After graduating from eighth grade, I began my high school studies in 1938. All was not new and exciting, as I mentioned, because the school administration moved Mrs. Peevey, my junior high math teacher, into the high school, along with Mr. Charles Gates, the history teacher and principal, and Mrs. Irick, the art teacher. Nonetheless, there were new teachers for me to meet (Miss Henrietta Perrin, home economics; Jonel Condron, librarian; and A. S. Jackson, earth science). In physical education class I must have learned a few things about the need for flexibility and creative use of space that I would use as a teacher in the future. Since the boys had the primary access to the basketball courts in order to prepare for their games, the girls were relegated to the football field to practice archery or, in bad weather, to the long, narrow front hallway of the gymnasium for arts and crafts. In order to utilize the time and space efficiently, Miss Linne Gilmore had us do a variety of things: building a small frame onto which we wove hot pads with yarn and carving a bar of white soap into a miniature replica of the Alamo. It is small wonder that on those occasions when we had access to the gymnasium floor I was delighted to play volleyball.

While I was able to wind yarn around the nails of the wooden frame to create an acceptable hot pad, my carved soap replica of the Alamo looked more like the mission after it had been overrun by Santa Ana's troops than in the shape that members of the Daughters of the Republic of Texas would approve. My handiness, I am sorry to say, extended into the home economics class as well. While my teacher, Miss Perrin, was very patient with us, my forays into homemaking left much to the imagination. After making fried bananas, which we had never made at home—straight out of the peel was good enough for us—I left the gooey mess I had produced on the plate, while my classmates eagerly dug into their creations.

While I would later master sewing buttons onto fabric, making an entire dress was quite another matter. After Miss Perrin had told me to even up some of the pieces that I would put together for the dress, I cut the wrong pieces short, having mistaken which seams would be where, and wound up with a zig-zaggy dress. The teacher recut the fabric so that the seams would match and produce an even bottom hem, but the result was a shorter dress than most girls were wearing in the late 1930s in Throckmorton. My mother, seeing the finished product, was horrified that I had wasted so much material. My grandfather chuckled when he saw it.

"Where did you get that?" he asked. "In See-More?" The town of Seymour, Texas, is thirty miles north of Throckmorton, and Grandfather took full advantage of its rhyming possibilities with his little joke.

I enrolled in home economics class again my sophomore year and learned to sew buttons on fabric—a useful skill—and plan menus and prepare meals. In order to gain an additional credit, I enrolled in an independent study homemaking class in which I had to plan and prepare thirty meals at home for the family. No one wound up sick; I gained my credit and learned a bit more about cooking. I did not, however, enroll for a third year, figuring my talents were to be found elsewhere.

In my junior year I took typing and bookkeeping with two different teachers (Margaret Preston and Katherine Medder). Here were subjects and skills that I understood and at which I excelled. In fact, during study hall in the library I became the resident expert, explaining concepts such as debits and credits and so on. My classmates to whom I provided these informal tutoring sessions "got it" and, much to my dismay, asked the business teacher during the following class session to let me explain a difficult concept to the rest of them. My abilities in biology class were another matter. Mr. Jackson, the teacher and his wife, attended the Methodist Church, as my family did, and so when I realized toward the end of the year that my grade was on the borderline, I persuaded my mother to let me bake a cake and take it to the Jacksons as a not-so-subtle plea in my defense for ignorance of biology. The home economics class had paid off after all! And I did pass biology.

Like many of my classmates, I learned to drive at an early age and began doing so, at perhaps an earlier age than some. Because of my grandmother's poor health, my grandfather, who was working at the farm during the day with my mother, asked the local judge to provide me, at age twelve, with a driver's license, for local driving only, so as to provide transportation for my grandmother. By my later teenaged years I was an experienced driver and delighted, when I had the chance, to take a couple of friends in the family car and ride around town. I recall outings with many friends and classmates, including Modena Raper and Eula Mae Cook, as well as encountering others who would be riding around, such as my classmate Glenn McWhorter with his buddies. Not surprisingly, these outings included stopping at various points to visit with other boys and girls out riding around. By the time twilight and then "dark-thirty" arrived, a game of "chase" might ensue.

One morning a local rancher, Edgar Tudor, stopped my mother on her way into the post office.

"Rena," he said, "you should know that last night Minta Sue and her friends went sailing around the corner by our place so fast that Jessie Maude [his wife] and I were afraid they were going to end up in our living room!"

My mother paused with the faintest smile on her face.

"You're telling me nothing I don't know, Edgar," she replied. "Who do you think was in the back seat praying we would make it around that corner?"

Curiosity had gotten the better of my mother on that occasion, and when my cousin Madeline suggested going for a ride, both Mother and I joined her.

Social time also included the M.Y.F. (Methodist Youth Fellowship), which sometimes involved travel with our local youth group to the nearby town of Albany for a district meeting. I met my first serious boyfriend, a senior named Johnny, in Albany in the year following the popular song, "Oh, Johnny, Oh." First written in 1917, the song was made a real hit by the Andrews Sisters with Glenn Miller & His Orchestra. Johnny and I dated on and off through college and in 1945, until another fellow caught my eye.

My senior year I took shorthand and advanced typing, enjoying both, and decided that I wanted to major in business when I went to college. My course in civics was taught by the superintendent, Mr. Rice, who must have had a great deal of administrative business to which he needed to attend because he chose often to conduct class from his office, utilizing the intercom system in our classroom to lecture and to call on us for responses.

"Now, Miss Thompson," his voice would boom over the speaker, and I would quake wondering which difficult question he might ask. By the end of the year I had gotten to know him better and was not so timid around him.

Commencement exercises for my graduation from high school were held Thursday evening, May 22, 1941, seven months before events at Pearl Harbor would propel the United States into war. The program I saved from that night indicates that the ceremony began at eight-fifteen o'clock for some reason. The class roll on the back cover of the program indicates that there were forty-two graduates; mine was one of the larger graduating classes. The program itself, titled "The Greyhound Spirit" (for our school mascot, the greyhound), consisted of four parts, each performed by members of the graduating class. Part I, "Self Realization," included sketches on "An Inquiring Mind," "Public Health," and "Recreation." Part II, "Human Relationships," included sketches titled "Respect for Humanity," "Cooperation and Friendship of Nations," and "Family Relationships" (in the last of which I played the role of Daughter). Part III, "Economics Efficiency," included sketches on "Occupational Cooperation" and "Vocational Guidance." Part IV, "Civic," included sketches on "Law Observance" and "Community Planning." After members of our class demonstrated our abilities in drama and oral interpretation, Part V of the program, "Presentations," involved the processional and presentation of awards and diplomas.

For a senior trip our class traveled on a school bus to Galveston and stayed at a motel on the beach. The forty of us who attended—we had started out as a double class in elementary school, remember—had a grand time swimming and playing on the beach. On the trip home we stopped in Huntsville, Texas, to tour the state penitentiary—a better plan might have been to schedule this tour in advance of our visit to Galveston, but we were a pretty good group and if the fear of God had not been instilled in us by the local churches in the previous seventeen or eighteen years, a tour of a penitentiary probably would not have done so either. Before the tour, one of the guides had asked our sponsor, in private, which of the girls in our group had a good sense of humor and could take teasing well. Sure enough, toward the end of the tour, the guide turned and faced our group.

"By the way," he said, "One of our inmates asked me to deliver a message to a family member of his."

Everyone in our group grew deadly quiet.

After pausing for effect, the guide said, "The inmate asked me to 'Tell Sally Sue, "hello."'"

Our classmate, Sally Sue Beatty, threw up her hands and let out a cry of distress. The rest of us howled and applauded. After we were in the bus and on our way home, the sponsor admitted that the "greeting" was a prank. Sally Sue flushed and said, "Well, I didn't think that the message could really be for me!"

In my sophomore year of high school I received my first permanent at a local beauty shop. My hair had grown long, and I decided it would be easier to manage for me and for my friend Marilyn Huston, who would sometimes come by and help me comb through it. So I scheduled an appointment with Mrs. Josie Neely, who had a shop in her home in the north part of town. As with other businesses, there were a fair variety of beauty shops from which to choose in the 1930s and 1940s in Throckmorton. Nell Rush and two other ladies operated a salon near the lumberyard. The DeLong sisters had a place south of the Henry Hext Grocery Store on the southwest corner of the stoplight. And Ima Hargrove and Gertrude Sullivan had a shop in Ima's home at the edge of town on the Albany highway.

After my sophomore year, my sister left home to attend McMurry College in Abilene, Texas. A nurse (Leona Lawson) came to stay with my grandmother during my last year or so of high school. Grandmother was bedfast during the last couple of years of her life, suffering from asthma and heart problems. After graduating from high school, I decided to stay home during the fall of what would have been my first year of college to help my mother and grandparents as my grandmother's health declined. As a postgraduate that fall, I retook shorthand and advanced typing, as well as English, as preparation for the courses I hoped to take in the spring semester at college. My friend Sallie Lou Tharp, who was also taking courses as a postgraduate, and I fell into the habit of stopping by the gymnasium during the first period of the day to visit with the coach (Anita J. Stewart), who had been one of our senior sponsors. Our first class did not begin until 9:30, and so we took advantage of our "flexible schedule" to do as we pleased. Before long, however, the librarian, whose study hall I was presumably supposed to attend during first period, reported Sallie Lou and me for this "infraction," and we were back in the principal's office. The principal these days was Miss Lera Irick, who had been my art teacher but was now elevated to administration while the men were away at war. She took us to task. I responded that I would be attending college in the spring, as well as having had graduated the previous May, so I was not quite sure how this discipline applied to me. Miss Irick sent me on my way, but the librarian had something to say to me as well. I would later learn to enjoy the company of our librarian as a colleague, but this encounter, when I was a feisty teenager, felt like a real affront. So from then on I did not arrive at school until 9:30 for my first class. And when my last class was over, I did not tarry but exited the school grounds, courtesy of our family car or pickup that I was allowed to drive in order to arrive home quickly, should my grandmother's health warrant it.

On November 17, 1941, my grandmother died. Mary Sue Parmenter was a pretty lady, and I fancied that I resembled her. Because of poor health, she had been in and out of bed throughout her life. In spite of this, she was like a second mother to me in terms of dispensing love and discipline in equal measure as deserved. If I did not know the danger of an untrimmed tongue, I certainly heard of it from a story my grandmother told about my mother, who as a child had sassed her paternal grandmother, who had moved from Bonham, Texas, in her last years to live with her son and his wife, Mary Sue. My mother was operating a sewing machine at this young age and just as she provided a retort to her grandmother, the needle on the machine went through her finger.

"That is good enough for you for talking back to me," the old woman remarked.

When I complained about some meal as a child, my grandmother prepared salt bacon and water gravy for the next meal. I ate slowly and with no enthusiasm but understood clearly the message: be grateful for the food that is prepared for you. My grandmother did not believe in wasting food. If a cake was not consumed quickly enough by the family and began to dry out, she would make a kind of creamy pudding to pour over the cake, now cubed and in a dish, bread pudding style.

My older sister learned a lesson from my grandmother once during laundry day. She would help my grandmother put the clothes into the machine and then rinse them in tubs of clean water (and water with bluing in it too, of course) before putting them through the ringer. It was my job to hang the clothes out. My sister did not care for the way I placed the clothes on the line and said as much to my grandmother.

"All right, then, you go help her," my grandmother said.

Thus, my sister now had two jobs: helping wash and rinse the clothes and then helping me hang them out before returning to help Grandmother with the second round. I tried to learn from my sister's "lesson" and keep my critiques of others to a minimum.

Of course my grandmother was also jolly and a great deal of fun. She did not, however, care to take me fishing because my incessant talking scared the fish away. She loved to fish and had done so since a child in Christiana, Tennessee, a tiny community south of Murfreesboro. At that time, Mary Sue Broiles was the second oldest of nine children. Her father relocated the family to Clarksville and then south of Bonham, Texas, which was where she was living when she met my grandfather. Two of her brothers, Frank and Arthur, moved to California. Another, Price, moved to Throckmorton. There he met and married Myrtle Hale, whose brother Rafe joined with an old Throckmorton family, the Reynolds, when he married Ruby, the daughter of B. F. Reynolds, who had served as county judge and operated an insurance and abstracting agency. My great-aunt Myrtle and Ruby, like many sisters-in-law, had a strained relationship. Myrtle, a stereotypical German-American, had strong opinions and a demeanor to boot. Ruby's personality, however, made her an equal match for Myrtle. Myrtle's mother, Mrs. Hale, was a bit more sly. The older Mrs. Hale had acquired a parrot somewhere along the way, a parrot for which Myrtle took no pains to disguise her dislike. The parrot, having no doubt learned the name of its nemesis from Mrs. Hale, delighted in calling out each time Myrtle entered the house, "Myrt, Myrt, help, help. The cat's going to get me, Myrt!" If Myrtle had less than hospitable relations with her sister-in-law and her mother's parrot, she did kindly help my mother, who was not a skilled seamstress, in making or resizing clothes for our family. Her husband and my grandmother's brother, Uncle Price, operated the local cotton gin, and their two children, Vasti and Andrew Price, were cousins and dear friends.

My grandmother's older sibling, Will, lived in Oklahoma. The rest of her siblings were sisters (Fannie, Annie, Jennie, Alice), who mostly settled in Oklahoma as well. Aunt Alice, who lived in Lawton, found fun in everything. Aunt Annie, mother of my mother's favorite cousin, Eula Mae, married a Baptist preacher and thus lived in a number of different towns. Daughter Eula Mae (Van Horst), now one hundred, is still great fun and living in Frederick, Oklahoma, on her own. Aunt Jennie died young, and Aunt Fannie's daughter married a Native American. Oh, how we kept up with family in those days, attending family reunions whenever we could. I must have first met most of this extended family when I was eight years old and my mother drove my grandparents, sister, and me to Lawton, Oklahoma, for the day. A few years later, when I was eleven, my cousin John William Lilly helped my mother drive my grandparents, my sister, and me to Christiana (to visit the various Broiles), Chattanooga (to meet Andrew and Emma Bumpus and son Ben), Winchester (where we encountered Ben and Mabel Grizzard), and Murfreesboro (to stay with Nadine and Sarah "Broiles" Grizzard), Tennessee, to visit relatives of my grandmother, who had grown up in that area.

My grandmother's relatives in Christiana were tobacco farmers, and during dinner the first night we were there I could scarcely stay in my chair, so ill did I feel from the smell of tobacco on the men's clothes, their having just come in from work. After a sharp look from my mother, I stopped fidgeting and simply did not breathe for the rest of the meal. My good behavior was not to last. In Chattanooga, after taking the incline railway to the top of Lookout Mountain, I made sure to creep to the very edge of The Rock, at the encouragement of one of my cousins, in order to have my photograph made, sending my mother, I know, into fits of anxiety. We also visited the water projects in Chattanooga connected with the recently (1933) inaugurated Tennessee Valley Authority, which our cousin Andrew Bumpus, an engineer, had assisted in constructing. The Tennessee Valley Authority, or TVA, as every child used to learn in school, was a federally owned corporation, ushered through Congress by Senator George W. Norris of Nebraska, a progressive Republican, and signed into law by Franklin D. Roosevelt. Although such federally sponsored ventures are still controversial today, the TVA addressed many issues connected with flooding, the navigability of waterways, the generation of electricity, the production of fertilizer, and the need to help people in a region, many of whom were especially poverty-stricken during the Great Depression in an area in which many natural resources and opportunities had been depleted. There is something to be said for comparing and contrasting the anger in many people's eyes about government-sponsored programs and initiatives with the hopelessness and fear in the eyes of others when nothing is done. As long as the ship of capitalism, on which as a retired business teacher I am happy to be a passenger, is navigated by human hands, there will always be the need for a productive set of checks and balances provided by the government so that she is kept clear of disaster from the corporate icebergs that often appear.

So much for my view of politics. Now, what of religion? While our family was scattered among Protestant denominations, in terms of religion my own branch wound up as Methodists. Mary Sue Broiles had been reared as a Presbyterian; W. E. Parmenter, upon arriving in Texas, had become a Primitive (or "Hard Shell") Baptist. Imagine the potential for doctrinal discord between the couple even at the simplest levels: a Calvinist who believed in humanity's total depravity with no free will to choose, who were elected to salvation or damned for eternity, and an Arminian, who did believe in free will and conditional election to salvation if the sinner chose faith in Christ. What conversations they had about the predispositions of the Almighty while courting or in their early years of marriage, I have no knowledge of, but by the time they arrived in Throckmorton, theological disputes—if there were any—must have been set aside. As there was no Presbyterian Church, they joined the local Methodist congregation: Arminianism had seemingly won out over Calvinism for their practice of faith, but my grandmother, I expect, maintained her beliefs when they conflicted with the enthusiasm or doctrinal differences with the Methodists, under a veil of silence, as so many people do when politics or religion intrude on the daily business of getting by. My grandfather, on the other hand, was only too willing to engage in spirited conversation, even debate, with any visiting Baptist evangelist who happened to initiate a conversation about eternal life with him.

As Leota Pirtle reports in her history of our local congregation, the Methodists in early Throckmorton were served by a circuit rider, a preacher who would ride into town on horseback the first and fourth Sundays of the month. On the second Sunday he would be at the Parrott School House and on the third Sunday at the small community of Profitt between Throckmorton and Newcastle. These circuit riders were equipped with a Bible, a book of hymns, and the Methodist Book of Discipline. Early worship services were conducted on the upper floor of a stone building in downtown Throckmorton that also served as the Masonic Hall. Land for a parsonage was acquired in 1886, and by 1896 a mortgage for $400 was recorded. A number of years after my grandparents joined the Methodists, the congregation had grown to exceed the small frame building they had constructed. Commitments were made by my grandfather and other members of the church board in the late 1920s to build a new church, and, in an act of faith, given the onset of the Great Depression, the building was constructed in 1929. My grandmother questioned Grandfather's wisdom in pledging one thousand dollars to this construction project, but he explained that other members of the board had done the same and that he felt obligated to contribute no less. The families, the men and women, of the congregation pledged their money and also their service to ensure the church would survive and thrive. In the years 1934 to 1935 drought conditions caused the local lake to go dry and wells provided the only limited source of water. Ranchers, whose livelihood suffered from the drought, sold the cattle they could before the government stepped in to exterminate those that might carry disease or were unfit for sale. In the midst of such conditions, the congregation continued to work at paying off their debt. The Methodist women's group prepared meals each week for the Chamber of Commerce to raise money. On more than one occasion they were forced to borrow water from citizens to wash the dishes. By 1937 the loan was paid off and the church was officially dedicated. Even had our home not been located next door to the parsonage and church, it would have been ever-present in our minds and hearts. When the church doors were open, my grandparents, mother, sister, and I were present, a practice I would continue with my family, as well as serving in leadership roles in the church.

As her health allowed, my grandmother had been an active member. She loved attending services and singing hymns, such as her favorite, "His Eye Is on the Sparrow." Written in 1905 by Civilla D. Martin (lyricist) and Charles H. Gabriel (composer), the song was inspired by Mrs. Martin's friendship with a couple by the name of Doolittle, both of whom suffered from physical infirmities—the husband, a cripple; the wife, bedridden. I do not know if my grandmother knew this backstory to the hymn. If she did, it no doubt helped her appreciate it even more. But now, after suffering from years of poor health and a weak constitution, she was gone. And so with a heavy heart, but also with tentative excitement, I prepared to leave my mother, grandfather, and this small town that had been my world to pursue a college education.

CHAPTER THREE

Round-trip Ticket

E ARLY in January 1942 I departed, with my sister, for McMurry College to pursue my degree and begin a new life adventure. My great uncle, Wayne Parmenter, had attended McMurry back when it was a brand-new college in 1923, after returning from World War I and deciding to enter the ministry. Because it was a Methodist college and we had heard a lot about it at church, my family decided it would be a good place for my sister and me to study. Located in Abilene, seventy miles southwest of Throckmorton, McMurry, along with two other private schools, Abilene Christian College (where my husband attended) and Hardin-Simmons University, provided church-related higher education for the small west Texas city and surrounding regions. When I arrived, between the fall and spring semesters, most of the rooms in the dormitories were occupied. Rather than see my older sister and me split up in two different facilities, my mother encouraged us to stay in private housing just off campus. Mrs. Ruth Moore, a widow with a young daughter, rented rooms to a group of ten girls, who shared household responsibilities and abided by the same rules of on-campus residents of the college. Known by those of us who lived there as "The House of Ruth," the home, set on a side street behind the college, was not quite as wild as the home of actresses in Stage Door, but did serve as the site for a lot of fun. Because I was an early riser, my responsibility was to set the table for breakfast. I also received first dibs on the bathroom, as the other girls knew that I did not tarry when taking a bath but that I could be a little cranky when having to wait on nine other princesses who were not so conscious of the clock. Room and board was twenty-five dollars per month, or two hundred dollars for the academic year, a bargain compared to the on-campus dormitories (thirty-seven dollars per month). Tuition was set at five dollars per credit hour, which meant, for a five-course load each semester, a yearly total of one hundred and fifty dollars. In other words, a four-year college degree (tuition and room and board) at McMurry cost approximately $1,400 in the early 1940s. Like most students I worked on campus, three hours per week, typing questions and other text for correspondence courses offered by the college.

My first semester of college, I enrolled in shorthand, typing, English, history, Bible, and speech. On the second day of class the shorthand teacher asked me to read from an assigned passage. After I quickly read it aloud, the professor furrowed her brow and said, "Miss Thompson, this passage was not to be *memorized* but *read* to demonstrate your understanding."

"I did read it," I responded. "I took a year and a half of shorthand in high school."

The teacher left class to visit the main office to inquire whether I could receive three hours' credit for the first semester of shorthand. After taking a test, I was awarded three hours' credit, once I paid the fifteen dollars in tuition fees. The same thing occurred in the typing class; thus, thirty dollars later, I had six hours' credit toward my degree, was enrolled in the advanced shorthand and typing classes, and completed twenty-four credit hours in my first semester. The second semester of freshman English was a literature class with Miss Jewell Posey; my American history class with Mr. Willis required a bit more study; I will never forget my Bible teacher's ability to place a Coca-Cola bottle in his mouth, tip it up, his hands free, and drain the bottle within a couple of minutes. These exhibitions, witnessed by any number of us in the student center, persuaded us that Dr. Gordon was a man of unusual talents. He was not, however, as shrewd about human nature—particularly that of college students—as he ought to have been. Each week, he gave a quiz of ten different questions to each of his four classes. For the final exam, he drew from all these questions, expecting that some of his students would not have encountered some of the questions given in the other class sections. My classmates and I, however, compared notes with students in the other sections and discovered that our grades would benefit from collaborative sharing of the questions from each other's weekly quizzes. Dr. Gordon, we supposed, probably never encountered a passage in the Bible about how it is easier for a camel to get through the eye of a needle than for a teacher to create a foolproof exam.

In spite of joining in on our out-of-class cleverness to perform well on an exam, I was still pretty timid in my new environment and had never taken a speech class in high school. A friend of mine, Bill Adams from Georgia, who was majoring in communication, helped me prepare for each of my speeches and tests in the public speaking class, and so I finished out that first semester with pretty good marks. The speech teacher, Harvey Cromwell, passing through my hometown the following summer, stopped for a cup of coffee and encountered Mr. Ed Merriman, who knew my family and me well. When he learned that I had been a student in this man's class, he chuckled.

"Isn't she a mess?" he said.

"I found her to be a very quiet student who did her work," the speech teacher responded.

Mr. Merriman looked perplexed.

"We must be talking about two different people," he said, and later asked me, "What did you do over at McMurry to give people this impression of you?"

What I did not tell Mr. Merriman was that I felt more at ease in my hometown and from my first year in college had felt a bit homesick. Even by the spring semester of my senior year, when I wrote to my friend, Sallie Lou Tharp, that I was scheduled to serve as the mistress of ceremonies at the college Press Club banquet and later give a talk at weekly chapel service, I admitted that I was "scared silly."

The summer after that first semester I returned home to Throckmorton and worked at the county office of the State Agricultural Agency, completing an acreage project for the county. A photographer had taken aerial photographs of the entire county and it was now my job and that of the two other girls working in the office to measure the boundaries of each plot of land in the photographs and apply a formula in order to determine the total number of tracts of land and the acreage in each tract. This information provided the county agricultural agent (George Blackburn) with the data he needed to converse with farmers about their crop-raising and rotation plans when applying for state funds. Each photograph had been taken from the same altitude, and our job was to roll a small, metered device around the boundaries as marked on the photograph and then record the data.

With part of the money I earned that summer I purchased a portable radio and took great joy listening to some of my favorite programs, such as Eddie Cantor (who I characterized as "a scream" to Sallie Lou in one of my letters) and his NBC show "Time to Smile." My sophomore year in college I enrolled in Dr. Willie Mae Christopher's English class, Dr. Hozelhaple's biology class, Mr. Willis's history class, Miss Tate's math class, and E. E. Langford's accounting class. It was a particularly cold winter for Texas, even as far south as Abilene, where one day we had snow. My fellow students had been clamoring for the college to allow us girls to wear pants to class occasionally, and this day seemed to warrant it. Some of the girls asked for and received permission from the dean to wear pants to class. I, however, did not wear pants. I found my longest, warmest skirt and some wool hose and showed up for my morning biology class. Dr. Hozelhaple entered the room and, before beginning her lecture, surveyed the students. She walked up one aisle and down another before turning to face the class.

"Well, ladies, I see that a number of you have chosen to wear pants. It seems to me that Miss Thompson..."—she glanced in an approving way at me—"has found an appropriate way to dress for this day."

Oh, did I receive some dark looks from the pants-wearing girls in that class and some good-natured teasing about my "conservative" way of dressing later on. In fact, I had worn pants in the past—in Throckmorton. My freshman year of high school I proudly sported a pink "pant suit" to school one day only to hear a senior boy call out: "Hey, look at the fresh-

man who forgot to change out of her pajamas before coming to school."
And everyone did look, and I was embarrassed. That kind of reaction and
attention stay with you.

I would not have had the slacks had it not been for my grandfather, who
knew I was growing up. Having observed me one day mowing the front
lawn in my school gym shorts, he walked into the kitchen and raised the
issue with my mother.

"Mae," he said, using my mother's middle name as was his practice,
"you need to buy the girls some pants. Minta is out there mowing the lawn
in her gym shorts, and some old fool just drove by and nearly went off the
road turning to look."

So pants we had and pants we wore—but not often.

The summer following my sophomore year of college, I took my second required Bible course as a correspondence course and attended an
accounting course in an independent study format.

By my junior year I had declared a major in secondary business education and participated in student teaching at Abilene High School, an experience that involved my grading papers for the typing teacher to whom I
was assigned, not being allowed to teach any of the class sessions.

In 1945 I graduated after three years of study and was handed a blank
sheet of paper at graduation, having courses to complete the summer after
graduation.

McMurry during the 1940s was a small community, the campus on the
southwest edge of Abilene, with not much traffic. With the boys off at war,
the total campus population was probably around 480. At that time the
campus buildings consisted primarily of Old Main (the administration
and classroom building, containing the library as well); Gold Star Dormi-
tory for men; Boyce and President's Hall, with a cafeteria in the basement,
for women; a campus bookstore; and the gymnasium. Parking places on
campus were plentiful since the only students who had cars were the older men training to be preachers, who needed transportation to the small
churches they often served. Most of the faculty lived in the neighborhood
and walked to campus. When we students weren't studying or working,
entertainment options included a nearby skating rink, bicycling around

the neighborhood, taking the bus to Rose Park and its pavilion, with a jukebox, for a dance on Saturday night, provided one did not miss the last bus at eleven p.m., or maybe an excursion downtown to eat out at a Mexican restaurant and then see a movie at the grand Spanish Colonial Revival-styled Paramount Theatre. In my letters to Sallie Lou between 1942 and 1944 I often documented what movies I had been to see, characterizing most as "plenty good." There was *The Forest Rangers* with Fred MacMurray, Paulette Goddard, and Susan Hayward; *Orchestra Wives* with George Montgomery and Anne Rutherford and featuring some great music by Glenn Miller's orchestra; *So Proudly We Hail* with Claudette Colbert, Paulette Goddard, and Veronica Lake as army nurses in the Philippines; *Cabin in the Sky* with Ethel Waters, Eddie "Rochester" Anderson, Lena Horne, and Louis Armstrong; *Stage Door Canteen* (of course!); *Thousands Cheer* with Katherine Grayson and Gene Kelly; *North Star* with Ann Baxter and Dana Anderson, about the 1941 Nazi invasion of Ukraine; *Claudia* with Dorothy Macguire and Robert Young; *Cowboy Canteen* with a host of country and western musical stars like Tex Ritter and Roy Acuff; *Journey for Margaret* with Robert Young and Loraine Day, in which an American couple adopt children orphaned by the London Blitz; and *Air Force*, in which John Garfield and company arrive at Pearl Harbor in the midst of the Japanese air attack. Such movies, the plot of many focused on or related to the war, kept audiences ever mindful.

There were also plenty of activities on the campus. While in college, I joined a women's social club (campus sorority), Kappa Phi (sponsor, Mrs. Fred Reeves), and participated in initiation activities of polishing the members' shoes, ironing their clothes, and so on. I attended the banquet of a men's social club (Kiva) with a fellow I was dating at the time. At the time the banquets were held in downtown Abilene hotels, such as the Wooten or Windsor (Hilton) hotels. In my physical education class our teacher, Mrs. Estelle Thomas, taught us square dancing and then sent us out to Camp Barkeley, southwest of town, each week to teach the servicemen how to square dance as well; we were invited to an early Thanksgiving dinner as a "thank you."

Constructed and completed during 1940–41, Camp Barkeley served as a training installation for the army. Consisting of more than seventy thousand acres, the base had a population of fifty thousand at its peak. In 1944 a unit of 840 German POWs was housed in the camp as well. Although Camp Barkeley was closed in 1945, the nearby army air base became Dyess Air Force Base, which is still in operation.

During my years in college, I sometimes took the bus from Throckmorton to Abilene, via Breckenridge. Because Breckenridge was "wet" and sold alcohol and Abilene did not, some of the soldier boys would often take the bus to Breckenridge for a weekend. Since they were not allowed to transport liquor on the bus, they would be well lubricated by the time of their return trip to Abilene. I always made certain to buy my connecting ticket to Abilene from Breckenridge in Throckmorton, so I and the few other female passengers could board the bus first and sit up front. I kept my head down as the soldiers boarded the bus, not needing to be greeted forty times before the journey began. En route, I would hear many of these fellows sing songs they learned growing up in Tennessee or Georgia or Alabama. One of my seatmates, an older woman who taught at the base, told me one of her first jobs was to teach some of these young men to write so that they could endorse their paychecks from the military.

One of my college friends from Abilene, Willeen Harbor, regularly attended the dances at the downtown canteen, as did some of the other girls, and dated a few of the fellows as well. Not having learned to dance very well until my senior year (and figuring that square dance songs would not be playing at the canteen), I did not accompany the group. My invitation to the Thanksgiving dinner at Camp Barkeley came from a fellow from Long Island, and one with whom I had gone roller skating. By the time I returned from the holidays, he had been shipped out. Such was reality. On another occasion, my roommate, Joy Green, and I went out on a double date; my fellow for the evening was a lieutenant with a convertible! Although I went out on the occasional date with soldier boys, I did not let things get too serious, having seen the crying and heartache that some of my classmates went through when their boyfriends or fiancés were shipped out. Nor were there a great many fellows to choose from at college during these years, since most young men were off fighting in the war. The male population primarily consisted of older men who had returned to school to prepare for entering the ministry and some young men who had not yet been called into military service.

My final year in college, I dated a freshman who was two years younger than I (as I had completed high school and was completing college early), but when his time to ship out came, I turned down his proposal to marry.

"Let's wait and see where we are when you return from your tour of duty," I said.

Shortly after, I received a letter from him, letting me know he had married a girl he had been dating in Houston before he had shipped out. This kind of news throughout my life has always been welcome when it has confirmed a good choice on my part. I later joked in a letter to Sallie Lou about my former, younger beau having departed: "Guess I'll have to get me a soldier or a freshman. Believe I'll take soldier."

After "graduating" from college in May at the ripe old age of twenty, I still had two independent study courses to complete in July and August, so I was back and forth between Throckmorton and Abilene. During the summer, I also dropped by several schools that had openings for business teachers to see if I could get a job. At the last one of these interviews in Albany, the superintendent told me, "Miss Thompson, I have senior boys your age or older and I don't think you could handle the discipline." So that was that as far as teaching was concerned, or so I thought. Once I completed the final two courses for my degree, I heard from my cousin Madeline that the Liles Insurance and Abstracting Agency in Throckmorton had a secretarial position open. I had known Mr. Stanton Dow (S. D.) Liles and his family all my life, as they also attended the Methodist Church. When I sat down with Mr. Liles to ask about the job, he paused.

"Well, Minta," he told me, "I know that your sister has a good reputation as a hard worker, but I don't know much about you." He paused again. "I guess we will just have to try and see how things work out."

That sentence was a real motivator for me. I contacted his current secretary, who was leaving before Labor Day, and the two of us persuaded the county clerk to leave a window in the courthouse unlocked over the weekend so we could crawl in to do a crash training course on how to set up an instrument for preparing an abstract.

As in many parts of Texas, oil exploration exploded in Throckmorton during the 1940s. As John Leffler reports at the Texas State Historical Association website, after the discovery of oil in the county in 1925, production grew by 1938 to about 123,000 barrels. Although oil production would decline by the 1950s and even further in the 1960s, the commodity continues to provide a supplemental, if not primary, income to many farmers and ranchers. And in the heyday of the early 1940s representatives from oil and gas companies were eager to lease land in the hopes of finding big wells. Thus, there was a need for abstracting services. Because it was the county seat, Throckmorton's courthouse contained land records that abstractors would search in order to prepare a history of ownership and transfers that served as the legal documentation needed for the oil companies to proceed with drilling. As the new abstractor for the Liles agency, I would process requests from the oil companies by walking across the street to the courthouse and utilizing indexes and volumes of land titles and transfers in order to construct a history of the ownership of a given tract of land. Since the volumes could not be taken out of the clerk's office, I would take each volume to a desk and type a new copy of the instruments with four carbon copies for our office files. When I was down to the last carbon copy, after the others had been used for other orders, I would have to type the instrument again. Depending on the tract of land, such a process could take several days of typing. At the time, the going rate was fifty cents per page. Today the process occurs via copies of photo images and costs five dollars per page. Each Friday I would type index cards for the new instruments that had been filed during the week in the clerk's office so that our agency's records would be up to date.

Some days were so busy that Mrs. S. D. (Beulah Howsley) Liles would come down to the office to prepare the orders for the abstracts so I could spend my day typing in the courthouse. Once I completed typing the instruments, I would make an index of them, number the pages, and prepare a certificate of authenticity. I made sure, from the first days of my employment, always to arrive at the office before Mr. Liles did, to sweep the floors, and to have the doors open and ready for business at eight a.m. My hours were eight to twelve and one to five (or later) Monday through Saturday, with fifteen-minute coffee breaks at ten a.m. and three p.m. During these breaks, I would usually meet the abstractors from other agencies, Gertrude Condron (who with her sister Sammie ran Thorpe-Condron agency) and Ruby Hale (who worked for her father, Judge B. F. Reynolds, at the Reynolds-Hale agency) at the drugstore or café. We certainly did not discuss business to give away who we were preparing abstracts for, so we spent the time discussing the goings-on in town.

This work certainly made me familiar with land ownership in Throckmorton County and introduced me to some interesting businessmen from the area and the big cities of Dallas and Fort Worth. One day I came into the office distracted by a runner in one of my hose. One of Mr. Liles' clients from Dallas was there and said, "Well, you will have to get another pair."

"Not so easy," I replied. Even though the war was over, and with it, presumably, rationing, women's hose were still difficult to come by when one lived in a small town.

"By the time I am able to get to the city [and by that I meant Wichita Falls or Abilene], the locals have already bought up the available hose," I stated honestly, with no other thought in mind.

The following week when the gentleman from Dallas was back in town, he placed a box of hose on my desk.

"I brought these along to help you out," he said with a smile.

Mr. Liles sprang to attention from his desk nearby.

"Here now, my gal is not that kind of worker," he said. "She is paid for preparing these abstracts and does not accept gifts."

"My God, Stanton," the man replied. "I was just giving her hose because she was having trouble finding them. That's all it is."

But Mr. Liles had made his point; he was a good protector; and he did allow me to keep the hose.

Because of the long hours and one-day (Sunday) weekend, I had to find creative ways to get out of town to do my shopping. As I lived at home with my mother and grandfather, my expenses were few, and I had a little bit out of my paycheck to spend on clothes. Returning from a football game with friends one Friday evening, we noticed lights on in a store on the square in Haskell, Texas (thirty miles west of Throckmorton). We stopped and I stepped inside.

"Are you still open?" I asked.

"Oh, no," Frances Lane said with a smile. "We're setting up for the shoppers we hope to see tomorrow. But come on in and see if there is anything you would like."

I had just met the co-owner of a west Texas institution, Lane-Felker, a women's clothing store that opened in 1940 and stayed open for fifty-six years under the loving care of Frances Walling Lane and her sister, Mattie Muriel Felker, along with their colleagues Hortense Lees and Patsy Pate Cobb (Patsy's mother, Dovie Starr Pate, provided alteration services at the store). These women provided a special kind of service to their customers who drove, even flew, great distances to find the right outfit. Frances and Mattie Muriel made sure that they had the right outfit by traveling to Dallas, New York, and Paris on shopping trips and by knowing their customers, who they were, and what they liked. If not that evening, then very shortly after, I opened an account at Lane-Felker and visited the store whenever I had a chance. Because of my work hours, Frances and Mattie Muriel would keep the store open a little late if I wanted to drive over after work. After I was married, I had not had the opportunity to visit the store for a while. One day a large box full of clothes arrived at our home, special delivery, from my friends at Lane-Felker, who thought these new items might interest me. My husband was not pleased by this approach to salesmanship. "Send it back," he said. And so I did so, with an apologetic note. The next time my husband and I had occasion to be in Haskell, we stopped by Lane-Felker. From the moment we walked in the door, my husband was the center of Frances and Mattie Muriel's attention—and it was genuine—they wanted to get to know the husband of their dear friend and customer Minta. Wouldn't he like some coffee? What was going on in Throckmorton? Frances and Mattie Muriel were tag-team players; one would sit and visit with my husband, while the other helped me. And then they would switch. Well, that was that. My husband never had much to say about my shopping in Haskell again. He, too, had come under the spell of Lane-Felker.

During my three years at Liles Insurance and Abstracting Agency, I learned a great deal that would later help me in my teaching career about how to thrive in an office environment. I met and dated, for a period of time, a young veterinarian who had just completed his degree at Texas A&M and who had come to Throckmorton in his government job to check out reports of hoof-and-mouth disease among cattle in Throckmorton County. In the summer of 1946 Mr. Liles granted me a two-week vacation to go visit my great uncle, Frank Broiles, who lived in California. During one of his visits to Texas, he had told me that if I would come to visit him, he would send me the tickets. Uncle Frank was the younger brother of my late grandmother, Mary Sue Broiles Parmenter, and had moved to California with his brother Arthur in the 1920s to find their fortune. They landed in southern California in the Los Angeles area. Uncle Frank started a ship motor repair company in Glendale and found great success. Uncle Arthur, a bit more laid back, spent more of his time in his fruit orchard.

So I boarded the train in Abilene and followed the Texas & Pacific route through El Paso and then through New Mexico and Arizona before pulling into the Los Angeles Union Station. On the long trek across west Texas, I fell into conversation with two young men and a couple of elderly women who shared a sleeper car with me and with whom I had played cards. As the train pulled into El Paso, the fellows and I decided to explore a little bit. After all, the train was to be in station for thirty minutes! We walked up and down the streets and arrived back in time to board. We sat in the club car to talk for hours, it seemed, before turning in for the night. I remember trying to shush the young man, whose sleeping compartment was just below mine.

"I wonder what your mother would think if she knew you had a man sleeping under your bed," he said with a grin.

The next morning, the elderly ladies, who must not have heard his comment, were delighted to see me in the dining car.

"Oh, my dear, you did manage to get back on the train. We were so worried when we didn't see you. We thought that you and those boys had been left behind in El Paso."

In Los Angeles my Uncle Frank and Mary, the woman he was dating, made sure that I had a good time. When I arrived at the house with Uncle Frank, Mary and another young couple were waiting for us. After we had chatted a few minutes, the phone rang. One of Uncle Frank's employees wanted to know if I had arrived.

"Oh, yes," Uncle Frank said.

"Well, does she have on shoes?" the fellow joked, no doubt having his own perspective on Texans.

Uncle Frank looked around the living room at his lady friend and the visiting couple, all of whom were stretched out comfortably.

"As a matter of fact," he said, "she is the only one in this house with her shoes on!"

During my visit, Uncle Frank and I went out to dinner and dancing at the Sky Room in the Long Beach Hilton Hotel, to the Hollywood Bowl to see fireworks, to the planetarium, to his cabin at Big Bear Lake, and on an excursion to Catalina Island, where Uncle Arthur's wife, Aunt Vina, not so helpfully provided me with a milk of magnesia tablet to prevent me from being sick. The ride over to the island was fine, but on the way back, the pill had its unintended consequences and I was sick to my stomach. In spite of the ride home, the island itself was great fun with tours and exotic animals. The two weeks flew by, and once more I was Texas bound.

Emboldened by that trip, I joined some of the local girls who worked downtown (Eula Mae Cook, Elizabeth Rogers, and Mildred Carter) for a fast weekend trip, in Mildred's car, to Carlsbad Caverns in New Mexico. With the birth of my oldest nephew, I drove my mother and grandfather down to San Antonio to visit my sister, her husband, and the new baby, John Michael, on some whirlwind weekend trips as well, departing Saturday afternoon after business hours and returning Sunday night. My friend Adrienne Smith had married and started teaching; my friend Billie John Grable had married and moved away; Marilyn Huston had joined the WAVES during the war; and, of course, my faithful correspondent and friend Sallie Lou Tharp had completed her schooling in Arizona and had begun her career as well. College friends such as Blanche Hooks, who married classmate Frank Turner, were well on their way to settling into a life as well. And I? While I enjoyed working at the Liles office, I kept hoping that a teaching position would become available in my hometown so I could put my business education college degree to work in a new way. So it did.

A month before I was to begin my teaching career, I resigned from my position at the Liles agency in order to drive my mother and grandfather up to Illinois so that my grandfather could find and visit the grave of his father. After two days on the road, we arrived in Springfield, where we visited the capitol and then stopped in a small town on the way to Jacksonville to inquire of a cousin (Benton Buchanan) about the location of the grave. We found the grave, with a few others, in a pasture, having been directed there by an old woman at a farmhouse. We took a photograph of my grandfather beside his father's grave, and before leaving, my grandfather gave the woman money and asked her to have a fence built around the graves so that they would be protected from wandering cattle. So far as I know, that visit to Calvin Eugene Parmenter's grave by his son was the last one that took place by a family member until my Uncle Wayne visited in the 1970s and made arrangements for the stone to be shipped to Texas for placement in the Parmenter lot in the Throckmorton Cemetery.

CHAPTER FOUR

What and How I Taught

H. P. Powers was a large-built man, about six-feet tall, with a square jaw and a level gaze. He had previously served as superintendent at McCauley Public Schools where my future husband had attended and later at Avoca Public Schools where my future husband had taught. From there he had accepted the position as superintendent at Throckmorton Public Schools and arrived in our small town to find that he needed to meet with his new business teacher. Earlier that summer Joy Pitzer, who had taught business for a year or so, had resigned in order to move to Dallas with her husband, who, now out of the service, had accepted a position in the big city. Billie John Grable called me down at Liles Abstracting and Insurance Agency to alert me that Joy was leaving. I wasted no time in contacting the school to inquire about an interview.

The interview was with Mr. Harry W. Rice, who had been the superintendent at Throckmorton since my grade school days. Much beloved in the community, he had been honored when the gymnasium and auditorium—a WPA project—was built in 1936 and he learned it had been named for him: Rice Auditorium. Mr. Rice was a jolly, heavyset man, who had decided to retire with his wife in Fort Worth. That interview had been easy and comfortable.

"Well, Minta Sue," he had said, "You are so young. I can't believe you are already out of college and ready to teach. I don't know whether you can handle this job or not, but we will give you a chance." He presented my name and candidacy to the school board, and they voted to hire me.

So now I sat across from the new superintendent, Mr. Powers, who was sizing me up. Deliberate in his actions and in choosing his words, he would punctuate whatever he had to say with, "Well, ahhh..." as a means of gathering his thoughts before allowing anyone else to hear them. This was not my style of communicating. I was more likely to say everything I needed to say at once, like a west Texas cloudburst. I explained what I had studied in school and my business experience downtown as quickly and persuasively as I could. I waited, an eternity it seemed, before he got to his main concern.

"Well, ahhh, Miss Thompson," Mr. Powers began, "you realize that as a hometown girl you might have a bit of trouble with discipline where the students are concerned."

I nodded, but I am not sure that I completely agreed.

"I would recommend that you begin the year by being very strict with the students. Do not let them call you by your first name. If they do, give them five demerits. You are familiar with the demerit system, I assume?"

I was not. There had been no demerit system under Mr. Rice's leadership. Mr. Powers proceeded to explain.

A demerit was a mark that a teacher assigned to a student who misbehaved. One demerit might be assigned for speaking out of turn; another might be assigned for tardiness to class. Students could receive demerits in any class, and the total could run up quickly. When a student accrued ten demerits, he or she was suspended from school for three days. A student could subtract demerits from his or her tally by spending fifteen minutes per demerit in detention hall, which was held each day during the noon hour and supervised by teachers, who shared the unhappy task. Boys had the additional option of receiving two "licks" by a board paddle from the principal to remove a single demerit.

For the decade that Mr. Powers served as superintendent, the demerit system checked the behavior of Throckmorton school students. When the next superintendent took office, the system disappeared.

So demerits it was. And I began my teaching career, the following day after that interview with Mr. Powers, determined not to have him or anyone else wonder about my ability to maintain discipline in the classroom.

✳ ✳ ✳

The first test came on day one in bookkeeping class. Buddy Putnam, a neighbor from across the alley of my family's home who was only a few years younger than I, walked into class and said, "What am I going to do? I can't call you Miss Thompson." And he was right. He and his brother and sister had come over to play with my sister and me during our growing-up years.

I looked at him and thought of Mr. Powers.

"Well, you have to," I replied, "or you will get five demerits."

He nodded, but the next day he came into the classroom smiling and said, "Could I call you 'Teacher' or 'Teach'?"

I gave him permission, and he called me "Teach" as long as he lived.

Buddy was one of a group of twelve boys (Matt Halbert, Garland Byrd, Louis Robinett, Cecil Ingram, Billy Massey, Terry Rice, Bonnie Bell, Curtis Cook, Clyde Denham, Kenneth Noles, and Andy Howsley) who dropped out of English IV during their senior year in order not to be eligible to graduate. All of their birthdays fell on the calendar in such a way that they were eligible under the rules to return for a fifth year to play football. And so they did. Having completed their required courses, they chose to sign up for all the business subjects: typing, shorthand, and bookkeeping. It was the largest class of young men in shorthand that I would ever have. As they were all good students, however, it was a real pleasure. Many of them planned to attend college, and they recognized the value of learning shorthand for taking notes in classes.

My schedule that first year included Typing I (introduction—learning the home keyboard: a, s, d, f, j, k, l, $;$, etc.) and Typing II (advanced), Bookkeeping, Shorthand, and a study hall during a six-period day. For the first few years my classroom was on ground floor next to the principal's office. That was certainly motivation to maintain discipline and keep the noise level low. The school building, now demolished, had been built in 1912 and consisted of a lower level (basement), ground floor (although elevated by a high stair entrance), and the upper floor. Elementary school was conducted in the basement; the ground floor contained the administrative offices, chemistry lab, English classroom (which had windows situated to allow students easy egress and entrance to a little store across the street where they would buy candy and sometimes sneak a smoke), math classroom, history classroom, and my two business classrooms. The upper floor housed the home economics classroom and the library. In later years the business classroom would switch places with the library, so that the librarian, who was also school secretary, would have ready access to the administrative offices.

My typing classroom faced east, and my bookkeeping and shorthand classroom, on the opposite side of the building, faced west. The same was true when I moved upstairs several years later. With shorthand and bookkeeping classes scheduled in the afternoon, there were many warm days for students and teacher alike. Once we opened the windows we discovered the ledges had made a good location for bird nests, and our boys often grabbed any unattended eggs to crack open on each other's heads. Open windows, no matter how high they were raised, could not cool the room, especially once we were on the top floor. So I asked permission to install a water-cooled ("swamp cooler") air conditioner that I bought in that west classroom, not thinking about the effect. My classes, which had always been full, were now extra popular. Students who wanted to sign up for a "cool" afternoon class were angry when the administration would not allow them to enroll once the twenty-four seats were filled. In the fall and winter it was a different story. Because the building was older, the windows would rattle when a cold front would blow through, and students would wad up and stuff used paper in the cracks to eliminate the noise and the cold air. When the weather warmed up again and we opened the windows, paper would fly everywhere and I would set the students to the task of collecting it.

The other feature of my classrooms consisted of ready egress. Both the east and west sides of the building contained fire exit slides attached to one of the windows of each of my classrooms. A number of years later, I had sat down at my desk to check papers for the students while they were completing a typing exercise. My normal practice was to circulate about the room while students were working in order to provide help. On this occasion, however, I sat down to grade and slipped off my shoes. At some point I realized I should get up and check on the students' progress. My shoes, however, had "walked off." The students, noting that I was looking down under my desk, began to laugh.

"Who took my shoes?" I asked with as straight a face as possible. More laughter. No response.

"All right," I said to the three boys sitting on the front row and likely candidates for the shoe theft. "One of you can go retrieve my shoes."

"Kenneth Don Boland did it," they called out.

I thought it was more likely John Ike Martin, but nodded solemnly.

"Kenneth Don," I said, "go get my shoes."

As he started toward the door, I shook my head.

"Oh, no," I said. "Someone downstairs will wonder why you are leaving the building. You may exit via the slide, the way my shoes did, and return that way too."

And he did. He took off his shoes to slide down the slide and retrieve my shoes. On the way back up the slide, however, his sock feet slipped and slid. In order to gain traction, he had to take off his socks. The slide, of course, was hot and he lost no time in returning to class. Unfortunately, he could not share his red, burned feet with the other culprits responsible for the disappearing shoes.

Exterior slides and air conditioners notwithstanding, we did a lot of work in those classrooms. The typing classroom held twenty-four Royal Standard typewriters that were serviced by a typewriter repairman from nearby Breckenridge, who stayed in his job nearly as long as I did. I learned a lot from him about the typewriter as a machine and about its particularities. For example, keys on each typewriter would strike each ribbon with a distinctive force that made it fairly easy for me to detect a typewritten page from one typewriter in the room versus another. Although I was no Sherlock Holmes, I did figure out a few things that prompted some students to nickname me "Eagle Eye" for my ability to discern when a student turned in homework for another, based on the machine that was used, since each student was assigned to a particular typewriter. Or I might notice that a student had used an eraser to correct his or her typewritten work, which was prohibited during the first semester.

I made certain that students took care of their typewriters as well. During one year when I took off a semester after the birth of my second son, I heard from the typewriter repairman that summer about the problems he encountered: chewing gum, bits of paper, and so on stuck in the basin where the keys were located. I was working at Liles Abstracting and Insurance Agency for the summer when he stopped by to share this news.

"Never were the typewriters in such a state when you were teaching," he said.

And the following year, when I was back in the classroom, I made sure that the typewriters stayed clean and in good working condition.

Regardless of condition, however, the typewriters could not always control what students might type. Fingers slipped off the home keys and the litany of "asdfjkl;" became something else altogether. Typing is different from playing the piano, but resembles it in some ways. The goal is not to look at one's hands or the keys. A wall chart of the keyboard was another matter. In an age before the concept of "multitasking" became popular, learning to type represented a number of different actions coming together. Students needed to keep their fingers on the home keys (wrists arched); reach beyond the home keys to strike keys on other rows; recall when to shift for upper case or an alternate symbol; apply sufficient pressure to the key to ensure a solid strike of key to inked ribbon to paper; listen for individual letters called out by the teacher—at first routinized, then alternating; remember to lift the left hand from the keyboard to advance the carriage lever to take the page to the next line; and, ultimately, read from a textbook first words, next sentences, then paragraphs, and find and strike those keys. All of these motions, maneuvers, and cognitive acts needed to come together in a rhythm, with accurate results, that could then be perfected in its speed. Once the students mastered the keyboard and began building fluency in typing from a text and, later, speed, they sometimes strayed from their assignments. In one case, it was to express frustration. While quietly circulating around the classroom one day, I noted that one student was typing, not from the assigned text in the book but, rather, a letter to the Almighty.

"Dear God," the note began, "please help me out..." She then proceeded to tell what she would like to see happen to me.

"I don't think God can help you out with that," I said quietly. She jumped, whirled around, and nearly knocked the typewriter off her desk. After that, so far as I could tell, she turned to prayer, rather than typing, for her communications with God.

Sometimes, of course, the students used my walking around the room to their own advantage. Passing by Ted Wright's desk one day, I heard him say, "Mrs. Cypert, you have something running up your leg." I turned quickly to look (I learned not to do so afterwards) and saw that I had a runner in my hose. I must thank Ted, however, because in the future I always kept spare hose in my desk drawer for just such emergencies.

Learning to type, of course, can be a frustrating process. To ensure that typewriters did not get knocked off their tables, I informed students that any damage to the machine of that sort would be their financial responsibility. Not surprisingly, we had no accidents. The students' own language, in later years, was another matter. In the late 1960s I observed some younger high school students who felt pretty free to express expletives in the hall, out of teachers' hearing, they supposed. I figured that such "talent" might find its way into my typing classroom when those students became juniors and seniors and eligible to enroll in typing class. I armed myself with a new policy and "equipment."

On our family vacation the following summer, I collected unused, still in the wrapper, soap and took it to school the following year. On the first day I announced that I understood that typing could test one's patience but that was no reason to use curse words and held up one of the bars of soap. The students chuckled, probably thinking that their teacher, fast approaching middle age, was turning into a senior citizen who believed in washing dirty mouths out with soap. These were the late 1960s and quickly 1970s, after all! Who would believe a teacher would wash out a student's mouth with soap?

No one as it turns out. Barely a week or two into the semester, one of the boys slipped on the keyboard and typed a wrong letter. Then out came the word, loud and proud. I looked at the student. Everyone else looked at me. I motioned for him to come forward, and as he did, I unwrapped the little bar of soap.

"You know what to do," I said.

He took the bar of soap and took one lick. He made a face.

"Is that enough?" he asked.

"Yes," I replied. "Now you can go get a drink of water."

Relieved, he walked down the hall. He returned a few minutes later with a crestfallen look.

"When I took a drink of water, the soap on my tongue foamed up," he said. "I shouldn't have taken a drink."

"Probably not," I replied, as the class hooted. "And you shouldn't have said that word either."

In later years I had a student, Sammy Cook, who would sneeze and say, "Ahhhhh sh--." I warned him that was no way to get by my rule, so I did use the soap on him several times. He learned to rub the soap off before getting his drink of water and that way he did not have so many bubbles to get rid of. One day, after his "sneeze," he got under his desk to escape the soap. When he looked out, there I was on my knees waiting and soaped his mouth good. After that he decided I meant business and was very careful when he sneezed and spoke.

Of course that was not the last time that a bar of soap was unwrapped. And, for the most part, the students watched their tongues.

By the mid- to late 1960s the school allowed me to purchase two electric typewriters—IBM Selectric. Although electric typewriters had been around since the beginning of the twentieth century, they did not become commercially viable until the 1920s and 1930s. Even so, it was the introduction of the IBM Selectric in 1961 that caught my attention, and that model really captured the market for the next couple of decades. Of the approximately twenty-five typewriters I had, all but two were standard. I required students to exceed thirty words a minute, with 100 percent accuracy, before they could use the electric typewriter. Each year the school allowed me to add two electric typewriters, and by the end of my career more than half our typewriters were electric. Even so, I would switch the students to a new typewriter each six weeks to ensure they understood that each typewriter (and keyboard) has a different feel to it.

Around the Christmas holidays I would often allow students in the advanced typing class to create pictures utilizing patterns of different keys on the keyboard. It is amazing, though probably not surprising, the image a whole quarter page of capital Ses can create when combined with other letters in upper and lower case.

This "artwork" also came in handy for the school newspaper, which I sponsored, titled *The Kennel*, in honor of our mascot, the Greyhound. Typing II students learned a bit about journalism as well as formatting columns, spacing, centering titles, and so on, often assisting with text in the school yearbook as well. Some of the articles and columns in the school newspaper invited creativity and gossip on the students' part: "Orchids and Onions" provided contrasting statements about likes and dislikes of various happenings around school; "Would You Like to Date This Boy/Girl" allowed the student author(s) to create a composite "dream date," drawing on various features (hair, eyes, brains, sense of humor, etc.) from different students within the school; "Meet the Seniors" introduced individuals within the graduating class throughout the year via some of their favorites (food, actors/actresses, even teachers); "Class News" and "Club News" gave the secretaries of these groups a role to fulfill; and, of course, "Sports News" took up much of each issue. Sadly, *The Kennel*, which had been around even when I was a student, is no longer published (even though it was never in the doghouse with the school administration).

Although some young men might have been reticent about taking a typing class, claiming that they did not plan to be secretaries, most would return to homecoming events relating how much their skill in typing had helped them in their careers. Students who served in the military in the Korean and Vietnam wars shared with me in later years how their ability to type kept them out of the foxholes and harm's way.

Of course, in addition to my typing classes I also taught bookkeeping and shorthand. From his earliest days my younger son was frustrated by his inability to read my Christmas shopping lists, written, naturally, in shorthand. Likewise, when I sat with a teacher colleague of mine who also knew shorthand at faculty meetings, we would often write notes to one another in shorthand, baffling jealous colleagues and keeping our thoughts safe from any curious administrators. The business of teaching shorthand, however, was quite serious. The young (mostly) women who took the class knew that their skill in this transcription system would have a great deal to do with their future success in the business world.

Although shorthand today may seem to be a lost art, it has a long history. One of its related words, stenography, comes from two Greek words (*stenos*, which means "narrow," and *graphe*, which means "to write"). Early examples of stenography, or abbreviated writing, are found carved in stone in ancient Egypt and Greece. Other parts of the world, such as Asia, have developed their own shorthand forms as well. The form of shorthand that I taught in schools was developed by John Robert Gregg in the late nineteenth century. While some earlier shorthand systems had distinguished between thick and thin lines, Gregg's shorthand used the same thin lines but distinguished among the phonetic sounds its characters represented by, for example, the length of the stroke. Gregg's semiscript system is international in its origins, drawing on earlier systems in England and Germany. Although Gregg's system was first published in 1888, it went through numerous printings, and by the time I began teaching in 1949 a Simplified version of it, thanks to the advice of shorthand teachers, had been published. An even simpler form of the Simplified version was published in 1963, and it was further simplified in the version published in 1978. In the shorthand class, students mastered the basics of the system during the first semester and gained fluency and speed the second semester. Students in my shorthand classes needed to learn the system and reach speeds of sixty to eighty words per minute.

I prided myself in the fact that students who took all of my courses had little need of attending a business college, having already learned the skills (including filing and the rules and regulations of insurance) that would help them obtain and keep a job. One of the life lessons concerned professional etiquette and dress. Fridays were business dress day for the young women in my shorthand class, who came attired as though they were going to work—and they were and did, in my class, in positions in the local community and around the state and nation. Even so, many of the students had physical education class right before shorthand and would need to be reminded by their classmates to zip up, rebutton, or make other adjustments following a rubric I created for students to check each other's professional appearance. Many local graduates returned to enroll in the class, as well as in bookkeeping, to benefit them in their own careers. Their presence added a great competitive dynamic to the class and some real-world affirmation of the subject's importance. When Nel Rey (Daws) Coker returned to take bookkeeping, Sam Nacol scrambled to achieve a higher score on his papers and exams. When Ladelle (Liles) Boyd enrolled in shorthand to meet a church secretary obligation, the young women paid attention and picked up their pace.

Bookkeeping class, which, yes, did become accounting class, was an easy sell to a lot of students. During tax season, we practiced with the simple forms, and students were able to complete the process for their summer labor earnings. Early on in my career I had students complete the final debit and credit forms in fountain pen ink. After my oldest son completed his accounting degree in college, he let me know that ballpoint pen had become the custom. In those early years we did not have adding machines, so the students got plenty of practice in math. Gradually, some calculation machinery appeared, initially purchased by Mr. Hurley, our school principal, from military supplies left over from the war at army surplus stores. The first lesson for many students was the hardest: the distinction between debit and credit, which for some was as confusing as stalagmite and stalactite is for my younger son. Once they understood that distinction, however, we were off and calculating. My older son noted the challenge many of his college classmates, who did not have the option of bookkeeping in high school, faced in their first year of accounting. What an argument for the benefit of commercial subjects, as we called them back then, in the high school classroom. Not all students need or want to go to college. Many of these bright young people might own their own business or work in someone else's, however, and what a gift for them to have this knowledge. For example, I recall when my husband and I visited one of our former students, Bill Nacol, who owned a jewelry store in Louisiana, we were treated to a firsthand look at his financial setup based on what he had learned in bookkeeping class.

In bookkeeping class, by the end of the year, students were able to finish their own business case study project, completing all the forms and documentation and seeing how everything could and did add up.

If I seem to be a cheerleader for the subjects I taught, it is not only because of their inherent worth but also for the ways in which they enhanced the lives and careers of the so many wonderful young people I taught.

CHAPTER FIVE

For Whom I Taught

T HROUGHOUT much of my teaching career, I was elected by the junior or senior class as a sponsor, and so I gained a lot of experience working in concession stands with students and organizing other money-raising activities (magazine sales, etc.) to fund the junior/senior prom/banquet and senior trips. The seniors always had first choice of electing two teachers for their sponsors, followed by the juniors, sophomores, and freshmen. My first year of teaching, not surprisingly, I was elected by the freshmen as their sponsor. Each class would have an end-of-year party, so I arranged with the parent of one of the students to provide a truck, bales of hay, and, thus, a hayride to Fort Griffin State Park, south of town, for a picnic. One of the freshmen, Tot Richards, kept us all entertained with stories about his family, particularly his father, his Uncle Red, and his Uncle Ernest Marrs. We played baseball and picnicked and declared the event a big success.

That group of freshmen loved to play and interact with each other. Some of these students, who were in my study hall, were not enrolled in a physical education class because of their schedules. So I asked for and received permission to take them out to the tennis courts during that hour for exercise (Bill Thompson, Wayne Fant, Nedra Hibbitts, Mary Ann Ellison, L. G. Reynolds, and Nancy Jo Beatty). They played tennis, when they were not arguing about religion. It seems William (Bill) Thompson, who would later become my family's attorney, was honing his skills in logic early on with his classmates. His parents were Presbyterian when they arrived in Throckmorton, but they joined the Baptist Church and Bill chose not to attend. The rest of our tennis club, except for me, were members of the Baptist Church, and Bill delighted in challenging them on their articles of faith. Although there were no Catholics in the group, Bill felt obliged to defend the Catholic faith in order to get his Baptist classmates to retaliate with arguments that he skewered, with wit and good humor.

They were a clever group and clever as individuals, as I discovered when one of them, Wayne Fant, arguing about some matter, pronounced to the rest of the group, "Weeeelllll, I thought..." Without thinking, I responded, "Well, you know what thoughts did." Wayne blushed, grinned, and said, "Yes, ma'am, I do." I probably blushed a little myself when I realized that Wayne knew the rest of the old saying that I had heard from my grandfather: "Well, you know what thoughts did: laid in the bed like I did and %&*$@ in the bed like you did." I learned to control my tongue a bit, after that.

The senior girls, in contrast, were not initially so fond of me. My predecessor had been the yearbook ("annual") sponsor, and in the advanced typing class she had typically given an assignment to the girls and then gone to another room to work on the yearbook. This, of course, left the girls free to chat the hour away. I was not assigned to the yearbook, so, in contrast, I stayed in the typing room and required these girls to work instead of talk. In later years, when I would meet up with them in the courthouse and abstracting offices, they would ask me, "Now, Mrs. Cypert, why didn't we like you that first year?" In spite of my tough approach that opening year, they (Betty Ash, Virginia Parrott, Elizabeth Roberts, Vondell Martin, Rebecca Spain, Beth Key, Joyce Wells, Lavonne Glenn) became good friends of mine. And once they were in the work world, they knew I had had their best interests at heart. Many of the senior boys, as I have already mentioned, had returned for an extra year to play football and took my classes, having already completed the other courses offered by the high school.

The junior class were just starting out with their business subjects, so they had no expectations of being left alone to talk. They, too, were a lively bunch (Bob Bachman, Freddie Barrington, Tead Nichols, W. J. Stone, Flossie Sue "Totsy" Thorpe, Betty Ann Morrison, Carolyn King), and we had a lot of fun. One day they all came into class grinning and took their seats. It was not until I stepped back into the classroom after hanging the absentee slip outside the door that I discovered the source of their amusement. A photograph of me from my high school days was pinned to the bulletin board. A quick reaction was the only way to address the matter.

"Bob Bachman," I said, taking the photograph down, "I will get you for this."

The class laughed out loud.

"How did you know I did it?" Bob asked, half protesting.

"You are the only one who had a brother in my class, and thus you would have the annual [yearbook] from which to cut out this photograph."

My powers of deduction were not always accurate, but the students over the years certainly did their best to keep me on my toes.

My good relations with the junior class resulted in their electing me as their senior sponsor the following year. We worked hard to raise money (concession stands, bake sales, magazine and fruitcake sales) for a senior trip to San Antonio to see the Battle of the Flowers parade. We departed at ten-thirty p.m. on one of our school buses and drove through the night. With no twenty-four-hour service stations or cafés, the boys came up with a euphemism for a bathroom stop.

"Coach," they would call out to our colleague who drove the bus, "we really need to water the bluebonnets."

The girls and women had a more challenging time and a farther walk to find those bluebonnets.

When we arrived the following morning at seven a.m., we discovered that our hotel rooms would not be ready until eleven, so we left our bags and began seeing the sights in the clothes we had traveled in all night. After the parade, we visited Breckenridge Park, the Alamo, the Mission with the Rose Window, the Long Branch Saloon, and captured much of it on home movies.

Since we were in the big city with thirty students, we told them all to hold hands everywhere they went so that no one would get separated or lost. What a sight: thirty seniors and four young sponsors walking around San Antonio—even crossing streets—as a group holding hands! Some of the students must have gotten wind of those arguments Bill Thompson and his classmates in the class below were having about the Catholic Church because a group of students asked if they could attend Mass in one of the large Catholic churches. I took the ones who wanted to go, making sure we all had a hat or scarf to wear to the service, and the other sponsor took the rest of the students back to Breckenridge Park. Some of that group observed a "secretary" bird at the park and reported to me that they had observed my (the business teacher's) bird in the park. Upon hearing its name, I chuckled and admitted that I let it spend its time there rather than in Throckmorton with me.

On the way home we stopped in Austin and discovered that the state legislature was in session, so we called home to ask permission to stay so that the students could observe the politicians in action. We got an "OK" from the superintendent to stay away an extra night, but Jeb Cornelius had married Nedra Hibbitts, who was a junior (both were allowed to complete their high school degrees) and protested that he did not want to stay but to return immediately to his new bride. We promised him that if he would stay, we would allow him to ride on the back seat of the bus and smoke cigars all the way home. He relented; we got seats in the gallery, and the students were able to see state government in action.

The trip home was not without its own excitement. To occupy themselves during the long ride on a school bus without a radio, some of the girls and my cosponsor Laverne Keahey got out their cosmetics and made up the boys, completing the effect with scarves on their heads. When we arrived in Albany, close to home, one of the boys (Bob Bachman) offered to pull up his pant legs, put on a long raincoat and scarf, and parade up and down the street with his dolled-up features, speaking to each person he met. He did get some strange looks, but the delight of his classmates was worth it. I can still hear Bob laughing about it today.

It would be difficult to continue my story of my life as a schoolteacher without introducing my husband, Walter, who taught and served as principal in Throckmorton for thirty-three years. Walter was born seventy-six miles south and west of Throckmorton in McCauley, Texas, a small farming community near Hamlin in Fisher County. He attended Abilene Christian College and served in the Navy during World War II in the Pacific Theater, on the U.S.S. *Duxbury Bay*, a supply carrier. Upon his honorable discharge from the Navy, he completed his degree at Abilene Christian College and accepted a teaching and coaching position at Avoca High School, where Mr. H. P. Powers served as superintendent. After one year of teaching, Walter decided to farm some of his father's land for a year, but a poor cotton crop persuaded him to return to teaching. By this time Mr. Powers had accepted the position of superintendent at Throckmorton.

A series of events converged: Throckmorton needed to replace its elementary principal, who was not certified; Walter attended a football game between Throckmorton and another school held in the Anson football stadium near his home; my mother, my colleague Laverne Keahey, and I found seats behind the Powers in a crowded stadium; Mr. Powers encountered Walter at halftime and invited him to sit with him and his wife in order to ask him if he would be interested in the position; Walter came to sit with the Powers, and Mr. Powers introduced him to Laverne, my mother, and me.

Walter drove to Throckmorton for an interview the following Monday and was hired as elementary principal. The few single female teachers, I am sure, took note of the new single young man, but the high school principal (Royce Holland) and the coach (Peck Martin) made sure that I had the first (and last) date with him. We went to Wichita Falls to see the Texas/Oklahoma high school football game matchup and met up with some students, later colleagues and friends, on a date as well (Don and Sue Beach Sims and Tommy and Ladelle Liles Boyd). I met Walter's mother on her birthday, November 11, that same year. After Christmas, Walter gave me an engagement ring. The girls in Walter's seventh-grade class, who claimed him as their own, received permission to come upstairs to the library where I was supervising study hall in order to see "the ring."

We were married the following summer on July 22, 1949. At the ceremony, my little niece, Candy Sue, who called me "Auntie-Mommy," having spent much time with my mother and me, was fascinated by all the flowers and excitement in the church. As Walter and I kissed, after the exchange of our vows, little Candy Sue said quietly, "Auntie..." But the "Mommy" came out loud and clear, much to the delight of all in attendance.

None of the soldier boys I went out with or even the fellows I dated on a steady basis could have prepared me for Walter. He was one of a kind. Having grown up in a small community himself, he, too, was a home-town boy or would have been had he stayed in the Hamlin area. As his former teacher and class sponsor, Mr. Melvin Courtney, as of this writing 101 years old, put it at one of the class reunions, Walter was full of mischief and fun. Some of his female cousins recall retaliating when Little Walt had made a pest of himself by chasing him up a pear tree. As they threatened to follow him, he began pulling the fruit and chunking it at them to keep them at bay, sending them into fits of laughter. His creativity had waned little by the time he invited me to the farm to meet his parents, on his mother's birthday.

"Now I must tell you," he said during the drive, "my mother is a large woman and is very self-conscious about her weight. Please don't say anything about it."

"Of course," I said, my eyes wide. "I would never comment about such things."

"And my father," he continued, "is very shy. He probably won't say more than two words to you during the entire visit."

As we pulled up to the farmhouse, the door swung open and a petite woman, less than five feet tall, came sailing out of the house, followed by a man who began speaking a million miles a minute, inquiring about our drive, whether we had noticed how wet the fields seemed from the recent rain, whether we were hungry...

I turned to Walter, my eyes sparkling. "Walter Cypert, you are the biggest liar I have ever met."

That left my future in-laws speechless. Walter burst into laughter and began to explain.

As I met the Cypert cousins, I began to understand what an effusive, joke-telling, life-loving, prank-pulling family I had joined. The members of his mother's family, the Flowers, were welcoming, genial, and full of fun as well.

So, too, in our early years of marriage, would I learn that Walter loved to play. Upon returning from an evening meeting at church or school, I would find the house dark and cautiously walk through, turning on lights until he would spring from his hiding place for an embrace. Like young married couples, we also had our squabbles. After one, my temper prompted me to grab our box of silver, a wedding gift from my mother, and walk the block up to her house late in the evening. My mother wisely refused to let me in and told me to go home to my husband. When I arrived back, Walter had locked the doors, so I went and sat on the steps of the Methodist Church with my silverware and cried until Walter, with a guilt-ridden look, came after me. While drying dishes for me one evening, Walter decided to demonstrate the skill required to make a damp towel pop. A tussle ensued, I ran into Walter's elbow as he held the towel out of my reach, and I ended up with a black eye. The next day at school, the students all asked me, "Mrs. Cypert, how did you get that black eye?"

"Mr. Cypert hit me," I responded, and the students fell into gales of laughter.

"Oh, come on, Mrs. Cypert. What really happened?"

"I told you," I said, with the straight face I imagined Walter might display. But, of course, they did not believe me. Yet I had told the truth and avoided an awkward situation. And, happily, our silly little domestic scenes were never more complicated.

Walter's personality suited him perfectly for the demands of his position in our elementary and junior high school. As principal, he could empathetically remember what it was like to be a child and also draw upon his Perry Mason-like skills of deduction and questioning to elicit the truth from a child in trouble. While some students remember the discipline he doled out as principal, more remember his antics in the classroom, focusing his students' attention on the lesson by beginning class with an elephant joke, a rendition of one of the Ink Spots' songs, or some other little poem or ditty he had memorized in school as a child.

He enjoyed and understood the children with whom he worked and even stood up for them as an ally, as on the occasion when a representative from a state office pointed out to him that some of the children were turning in their lunch trays with food left on them.

"You and the teachers should make sure that those children clean their plates," she insisted.

"Do you always clean your plate?" Walter asked.

"Well, no," she stammered, "but..."

Walter continued, "We always ask the lunchroom workers to serve each student a little bit of everything so they at least have the opportunity to try it. But we don't force feed."

Sometimes, however, it was the children who made the point, which delighted Walter. When a representative from the regional service center, whom Walter had known for some years, visited the school, he and Walter walked out to the playground to watch recess in session. Suddenly, out of nowhere—as it often is with children—a little boy ran up to the two of them and kicked the representative in the shin and then disappeared as quickly. The representative, dressed in flashy red pants as it happened, grabbed his leg in pain. Once he determined the man was all right, Walter apologized.

"I'm sorry," he said, "but the color red really sets off some children."

Later in the day as they walked down the hall, they passed the same little boy, and, as the representative gave the child a wide berth, Walter stopped to speak.

"Say," he asked, "why did you kick my friend?"

The little boy looked from Walter to the man and back to Walter again. Tears welled up in his eyes, and in a quavering voice he stammered, "Oh, Mr. Cypert, I didn't know he was your *friend!*"

How Walter loved retelling that story, keeping his face as straight as he did when the child provided his rationale.

Walter had earned his master of arts degree in economics in 1951 from Hardin Simmons University after a series of summers in which we loaded our possessions for a move to Abilene. During those days, I kept busy taking coursework in such things as swimming, determined to better myself yet shivering at the prospect of jumping in that gloomy indoor pool with the cold water yet again. In the late 1950s it was my turn, and we spent several summers in the humidity of Denton, Texas, while I pursued and earned (in 1959) a master of business education degree at the University of North Texas (then North Texas State University), where my older son would decide to attend. Chuck was with us by that time, so Walter got to spend lots of time with his firstborn, creating "wolf stories" for afternoon nap time and finding other ways to keep Chuck out of the landlady's flowerbed and, equally important, out of the searing heat. I, meanwhile, spent industrious days, pausing only for pie and coffee breaks in the afternoon to laugh and gossip with my dear friend and fellow student Rose Marie Pilcher.

During the school year, my early married life with Walter was inevitably connected with our work as educators in the Throckmorton school system. Weekdays at school started between seven-thirty and eight and technically ended at four p.m., but many weekday evenings involved school activities: sporting events, clubs, and so on. Friday nights in the fall were devoted to attending football games, or selling tickets, or working in the concession stand, or, in Walter's case, running the clock. During rain or other foul weather, he often had a heavy hand on the clock. If we were not at school, we were probably thinking about school or talking about school and the many colleagues and students with whom we worked.

Although we did not start our biological family until six years into our marriage, we had children aplenty in the lives of the students with whom we worked. As a young couple without children but with a newly purchased home, we could provide a safe and fun space for the high school students to gather and enjoy each other's company. In 1949 I was again elected freshman sponsor and had such a sweet group that I sweated out sponsor elections every year for three years hoping none of the other classes would elect me because I wanted to stay with the class of 1953. Everything worked out for me, and I was their sponsor for four years and loved every one of them. We received permission early to plan a senior trip to

New Orleans, Louisiana, and how we worked during those years to raise money: bake sales, concession stands, work days, homemade ice cream sales—anything that would help us raise the $1,200 we needed to charter a Greyhound bus and to pay for motels and some of our meals.

It was this group that commandeered our home on many occasions. While I was still finishing work at school, they would go to our house and begin cleaning so they could have a party. Arriving home, I would find them in the living room, dining room, kitchen, and bedrooms, setting up tables for games. From seven to ten p.m., the students would play games, eat food they had brought or that I prepared, and listen to music.

On one of these evenings some girls came to me to tell me that they needed to use the bathroom but could not open the door. I followed them, knocked sharply on the door, and called out, "Open up."

I found four boys (Bobby Key, Jerry Bibb, Tommy Boyd, and Don Sims) in a circle playing poker and betting their oil wells.

"No games in the bathroom," I said. "And, house rules: no poker playing."

That was OK with them. They just found some space in another room and invented another game.

Their senior year was pretty special, and I remember so much about many of them. Tommy Boyd was the only boy who signed up for Typing II. Once he would get his lessons typed, he would come up to my desk, while I was circulating around helping students catch up, and put his feet up on my desk and read my newspaper. The girls fussed that they could not get by with the things that Tommy did, and I guess they were right.

Our senior trip to New Orleans started and ended with a lively bus driver on the chartered Greyhound coach, whose musical repertoire included a nonstandard version of "How Much Is That Doggy in the Window," and navigating abilities through the narrow streets of New Orleans that impressed us all. Our time in the Big Easy included a tour of the city, dinner at Antoine's, playtime at Lake Ponchatrain Park, and a nightclub tour of the city. For this last event the students had to obtain permission from their parents in advance. The bus took us to visit, but not participate in, the gambling casino and a series of nightclubs with shows, where the strongest drink for our group was a Coca-Cola or Shirley Temple, and the boys looked but did not touch. The night after the nightclub tour, the boys staying in the room next to ours kept giggling and I could not sleep, so finally Walter got up to go see what they were doing. Those boys (Tommy Boyd, Jerry Bibb, Teddy Wright, Don Sims) were dressing up like some of the women from the nightclub tour show and doing strip teases and having a great time.

Not surprisingly, when this group had their assembly program, they chose a womanless wedding. Tommy Boyd, the tallest in the class, was the bride and Don Sims, one of the shorter members of the class, was the groom. All the boys had fun stuffing their bosoms and wearing wigs. Don Sims was always creating excitement. For a Commercial Club program, an Easter parade, he wore overalls, carried an old stogie (cigar), and brought his dog. Nancy Jo Beatty brought her cat, which promptly jumped on Don's dog and pandemonium broke loose. The fur flew, and before everything was over, we had to clean up the stage after both animals dirtied it.

The class of 1953 took a vote and requested that the school administration allow me to sit on stage with them, turn the tassels on their mortarboards, and shake their hands once they received their diplomas.

New Orleans was quite the popular destination in the 1950s for senior trips. The class of 1955, of which I was also the senior sponsor, planned their trip, and we again worked hard to raise the money. Because I was expecting my first child in 1955, my physician, Dr. Harrell, recommended that I not accompany the seniors, so other teachers went along. This group took the train and had sleepers in a Pullman coach. Shaving cream, which had been introduced in 1949, was still a relatively new thing, so the male students certainly had to take some along—more for surprising their classmates than for shaving, so they told me after the trip. Unfortunately, as they related, with less than sincere faces, some of the other passengers on the train received a dose of the shaving cream as well. I expect that the passengers on that train were delighted to bid the class of 1955 farewell in New Orleans.

One other class selected New Orleans for their senior trip destination, and, while they were a delightful group, the resulting trip was one none of us would soon forget. I had been their sponsor for two years and thought a lot of them, but many things had changed in popular culture and in the world between 1953 and 1958—and students were a lot braver. After the high jinks of the class of 1955 on the train, the school administration decided that the class of 1958 would take a chartered bus to New Orleans. Walter and I accompanied the seniors along with Coach Bill Atchley and his wife, the former Mary Ann Boland, whose Throckmorton senior class trip had been to Mexico. While the tours and activities were the same, the after-party was not.

The students, it seems, were thwarted by the location of their rooms. We had been unable to get a block of rooms together, so the students were scattered up and down the hallway. Did they sneak down the hallway and furtively knock at the door of their classmates for admission in order to make plans for the evening? No, around eight p.m. they exited through the window, eight stories up, crawled along a narrow ledge past the hotel windows of other guests—guests who were changing clothes, guests who were startled to see young people crawling on the ledge outside their window, guests who called hotel security—in order to arrive at the windows of the room of their classmates.

Shortly after receiving these calls about ledge-crawling youngsters, or perhaps cat burglars in the minds of the unsuspecting guests on floor eight, hotel security contacted Walter and Bill, who explained to the students the danger of crawling on ledges as well as going past other people's windows. To the hotel security, Walter and Bill explained that the students were from a small town.

"They probably haven't stayed in a hotel before," Walter said in his most earnest voice. "They're just acting as they would at home."

The hotel security officers were mollified, if perplexed, about a community where ledge crawling was a normal activity, but warned the boys not to open the windows, much less exit through them.

But that was not the end of the evening. Whereas attending the nightclub tour had prompted a group of boys in the class of 1953 to re-create the event in their hotel room, twelve of the boys in the class of 1958 decided, after the window ledge crawling escapade, to slip out of their hotel rooms again—this time, fortunately, using the elevator. While three or four ventured down to the bus station to buy gifts for their girlfriends (Harold Keeter, Dale Hilley, and Fred Bruton), the rest set out to revisit Bourbon Street.

When hotel security spotted the same young men they had earlier scolded about ledge crawling leaving the hotel, they called our room around two a.m. to let us know. Walter and Bill set out to find them. Fortunately, the boys had stayed together and had settled in a bar. Walter caught their attention from the door and motioned them with a jerk of his hand and arm. The boys did not tarry but came outside immediately; one fellow was so scared he brought his shot glass with him. When he realized his error, he asked, "What can I do with this?"

"Set it down," Walter responded.

He tried to set it down on a fire hydrant without success, but his efforts provided a great deal of merriment for his classmates.

The news arrived home before we did. As the bus pulled into the school parking lot the following night, we observed many cars and many parents standing silently on the sidewalk. Evidently the administration had communicated that because of their behavior, some of the students would not be allowed to graduate. The parents did not take their children home, lecture them, and put them to bed. No, the parents, their children, the sponsors, and the administrators went into the school building for a meeting at which many speeches were given, many accusations leveled, and no little blame was placed on the sponsors, who were not allowed to speak. At that point, Brother Hana, a minister, whose son had been part of the Bourbon Street after-party, stood up and addressed the group: "We have trusted this school with our children for twelve years, and they have done a pretty good job. Why would we now blame them for something that the students did on the trip?"

Ultimately, the students were allowed to graduate, and their worst punishment, at school anyway, was fifteen minutes per day in detention hall for one month. When asked to help monitor that detention hall, I refused, stating that I had already served my time with that group. That said, many of the students in the class of 1958 would go on to become educators themselves and work in government and law enforcement—finding success and happiness in their lives.

After that trip, the school board and administration ruled that sponsors did not have to accompany seniors on their trips. I continued to work with classes to raise money for the trips, but I stayed at home. Some teachers did accompany students on their trips, but after a few more fiascos, the school board and administration ended out-of-state trips and then later ruled out three-day trips. From that time on, the senior class was allowed to go on three one-day trips. One of the first one-day trips I recall was a trip to the HemisFair in San Antonio in 1968. We left by bus at four a.m. and returned at six a.m. the next morning. I was in a different world for the weekend—I had never been so tired. We had walked all over the fairgrounds and had stayed for the live Bob Hope Show, which ended late, resulting in our early morning return to Throckmorton.

The other big event of each school year was the junior/senior banquet. Even when I had been a student, the juniors would plan a banquet, a grand meal, for the senior class, followed by a program of readings, speeches, and skits to celebrate the graduating class. When I first began teaching, I recall the banquets being held in the school library with the parents preparing the meal across the hall in the home economics room. That tradition continued until 1952 when the junior class decided they would like to have a prom so that they could dance. As class sponsor, I sent three of the students (Don Sims, Helen Nichols, and Teddy Wright) to meet with the school board to present their request. The board agreed, and in the spring of 1952 the first banquet and prom was held at Throckmorton High School. The banquet was still served in the library, which, as usual, was decorated. But so, too, was the gymnasium of Rice Auditorium, even if simply. The volleyball net was set up mid-court and decorated with paper flowers (made from colored napkins and tissue paper). The north end of the basketball court was available for dancing with an out-of-town band performing on stage; the south end of the basketball court had tables and chairs and board games available for those who did not wish to dance or wanted to sit one out. Parents were invited to sit in the bleachers and watch the young people dance, and, of course, plenty of teachers/sponsors were present. The event was deemed a big success, and from 1952 forward, the junior senior banquet and prom has included a dance. As faithful custodian of the building, Mr. T. K. Ball probably was not pleased that young people in dress shoes would be dancing on and scuffing up the gymnasium floor, but his concern was short-lived. By 1956, when the new elementary school was completed with a cafetorium (a kitchen at one end, a tiled dining area, and a stage, allowing for an auditorium), the junior/senior banquet was moved out of the gymnasium and Rice Auditorium and into the elementary school cafeteria, which provided a range of possibilities for banquet decorations that exceeded the gymnasium's volleyball net. The banquet themes and decorations, which attempted to create an elegant atmosphere far removed from the environment of our small Texas town, included such possibilities as a visit to outer space, a night in Paris, and a trip to Las Vegas.

In the years that I was junior class sponsor I would work with the other sponsors and students to prepare a program and decorate the cafeteria. In 1964 a home economics teacher and I were the sponsors.

"I am artistically talented," she informed me. "Since your talents are in other areas, you can do the program."

I agreed and then was determined that my program would match or exceed her art, so I went to work. The students in this class, as was most often the case, were a talented group, and since it was the year of the NBC television show TW3 or That Was the Week That Was, we decided to use that show, hosted by David Frost, as inspiration for our theme: That Was the Year That Was. It was also the year that the Beatles appeared (in February) on The Ed Sullivan Show, so one of the students, Karen Nichols, asked my husband, Walter, Mr. Hurley (the high school principal), Mr. Boyd (the basketball coach), and Mr. Neely (the science teacher) if they would dress up as the Beatles and pantomime to a record. Of course they agreed. We had live singing talent with Vannie Johnson performing. Four other boys, who did not have a role or great singing voices, formed a quartet and sang the school song. But the climax of the evening was the Beatles. When the curtain opened on Walter, Burton, Tommy, and Bob dressed up as the Fab Four (with wigs and Liverpool suits), guitars in hand or working a drum set, the students went wild. Before the crowd quieted, the needle was placed on the record backstage and "I Wanna Hold Your Hand" came blasting out with the faux-Beatles shaking, rattling, and rolling. When the program was over, the students continued clapping. They wanted more. They didn't even want the dance to start, so much were they enjoying the program. I had accomplished my goal.

The class of 1968 showed talents as juniors in 1967 that we didn't even know they had. Glenn Daws stole the show with his Will Rogers impersonation, and Johnna Davis turned out to be a wonderful torch singer, slithering up to Coach Tommy Boyd and sitting in his lap to deliver her song. The whole class provided a classic skit in which they imitated each of the seniors of that year. The banquet always included a reading of "The Class Prophecy" by the juniors, in which they imagined the future lives of their graduating classmates, and "The Senior Class Will" by the seniors, in which they assigned their various talents and possessions to the upcoming senior class.

Such shows were great fun, gave the students valuable experience getting up in front of an audience, and brought out everyone's creativity. Even after other high school classes and groups stopped putting on assembly programs, my Commercial Club continued the yearly tradition of putting on a program ranging from Christmas stories to Coca-Cola shows.

Shortly after I began teaching, I proposed to the students enrolled in my business classes that we form a related school club. I gave them the choice of forming a chapter of the Future Business Leaders of America, which would include dues to a state and/or national organization, or creating our own unaffiliated Commercial Club. The students chose the latter, and the Commercial Club met during the regular time for class organization meetings. Our meetings involved speakers (such as court reporters), discussions about the upcoming school newspaper, *The Kennel*, and initiating new members (requirements included taking at least one business subject) in a dress-up day (as cartoon characters and so on) that involved a march through the elementary school to show the students' creativity. For many years there was also an end-of-year Commercial Club banquet that included a short program or a picnic, often held at Fort Griffin State Park.

One year one of the boys (Curtis Timmons) jumped up to catch a baseball and came down holding his crotch. He had split the seat out of his new jeans. I always carried a little sewing kit in my purse, so I told him to get on the bus and hand his jeans out the window to me. I sewed them up, and he was able to continue playing.

On another occasion I was behind the batter calling strikes when the hind-catcher missed the ball thrown by the pitcher. The ball hit me squarely on the nose, breaking my glasses right in the middle. I had a black eye the next day and had to buy new glasses, but we still had a lot of fun. At another picnic, the park ranger came by to tell the sponsors that tornadoes were touching down around Throckmorton. Although the sun was shining at the park, we loaded the students up and drove back to the school. The parking lot was full of parents worried to death about their children. We had been lucky: no storms hit on the way home or even later.

During my years of teaching, I also gave birth to my two sons: Chuck in 1955 and Rick in 1961. When I learned that I was pregnant, I decided to resign at the end of the 1954–55 school year. The school replaced me with a first-year teacher whose husband was the new Methodist preacher at Elbert, a small town northeast of Throckmorton. They also hired her husband, the preacher, as a substitute teacher for the fifth-grade class, when that position was vacated. He began the 1955 school year doing his best, but the pulpit and the school desk did not always mesh, and he began each Sunday service by asking his congregation to pray that a permanent teacher be found for the fifth graders. Meanwhile, I had given birth, and, while motherhood was wonderful, I secretly missed teaching. One day the superintendent called and asked me if I was certified to teach elementary school. I contacted the college, and, although I had trained in business subjects, my education courses and certification were for kindergarten through twelfth grade. So, in October 1955, I placed my sweet son Chuck into the capable hands of my mother during the school day and began teaching the thirty-one fifth graders (seventeen boys and fourteen girls) for whom the Methodist preacher had prayed with his congregation.

Even though my temperament was better suited to high school students, I enjoyed this particular fifth-grade class and had no discipline problems.

During recess, I would jump rope with the girls and/or play baseball with the boys. I recall all the children fondly. Of the girls, I remember in particular Sandra Blackburn, Lara Beth Hext, Barbara Jennings, Sharon London, Sandra Nelson, and Zana Wright. Some of the boys whose antics I recall were Larry Balthrop, Corky Boland, Jay David Dunlap, Gary Harvey, Donnie Hibbitts, Mike Kline, Kenny Liles, Sam Massey, Jack McNutt, Mike Smith, and Tencil Scott. Several events occurred that bring these particular students to mind.

Barbara Jennings, for one, had a lovely singing voice. Several of the boys were teachers' kids, and Jack McNutt had a younger brother who would come to one of the two doors to make faces as his class had already been dismissed. I embarrassed Jack by saying, "Tell your folks about Terry making faces." Believe me when I say that little Terry did not stop by the door of our room again. Kenny Liles had an eye problem, so I moved him close to the front of the room, and his mother was worried about his grades while she was to be in Abilene giving birth to her daughter, Lisa. Kenny's father, Keno, helped him at home with his schoolwork, and Kenny made better grades those six weeks and for the remainder of the year. Corky was the leader of the boys in sports. Jay David Dunlap was the sweetheart. On Valentine's Day the students would pass out all their valentines one at a time. When Jay David's turn came, he presented Merlene Thompson, his girlfriend, with a small box of valentine candy, and the rest of the students really cheered. Zana Wright was a hugger, and I kindly had to break her of the habit. And, of course, there were so many memories of this group of students of whom I think so much. I had a wonderful year with these students, but by the following year, when the high school business teaching position became available, I returned to high school for the smaller classes, type of homework, opportunity to sponsor, and different style of communication with the students.

When Chuck was ready to enter school, I gave birth to Rick in March of 1961. I took maternity leave at mid-term (December 1960), and James Beach, a former student of mine who had just finished college, taught my classes for the rest of the year. By the time August of 1961 rolled around, I began teaching again, this time, my former fifth-grade students, who were now in high school. In 1962 the yearbook was dedicated to me. My dear mother provided childcare support for me. Both my sons loved Grannye and enjoyed spending the night with her when Walter or I had school responsibilities. In Walter's case it was running the clock at football and basketball games. I was either selling tickets or working with students in the concession stand as a class sponsor. While I mostly served as junior or senior sponsor, my colleague Laverne Keahy and I had a great time as sponsors for the freshmen class in 1947–48, a group we took to the swimming pool in Cisco, Texas. When I returned to teach high school in 1956–57, I was class sponsor with Mrs. Robinett, the math teacher, and we organized a class party for the students at the old railroad depot, which had become a youth center.

Sometimes you just know that the students in a particular class are going to create excitement. One year a group of boys petitioned for and received permission to take home economics class. The fact that the new teacher was young and lovely probably had nothing to do with it. The boys learned their lessons well, too. All kinds of wonderful aromas of fresh-baked goods drifted down the hallway. Such culinary art takes time, however, and by the time the goodies were ready, the boys had to report to their next class. The students in the home economics class during the next hour were all girls, and the temptation of fresh-baked goods was too much for them to resist. At first they would merely sample, but gradually they began to consume more, leaving little, if any, of the boys' "assigned work" available for them to try later in the day.

The boys were furious and determined to seek revenge. It came when the teacher introduced a unit on candy. "Let's make chocolate candy," the boys proposed, and their home economics teacher, who had done a bit of the sampling herself, agreed, delighted with the young men's enthusiasm. So she did not notice when, in the midst of their candy making, the boys melted and added chocolate-flavored Ex-Lax to the mixture. She did notice later, however, when she and the class of girls, who had refused to show restraint in consuming foods they had not made, once more finished off the chocolate candy. How long did it take? The next day, the girls came to school, having had a rough night. One girl in particular had appendix problems, which heightened the seriousness of the boys' offense.

The boys, of course, had to be punished. But the teacher, who seemed unable to employ classroom management strategies and to maintain discipline, was also called on the carpet. During the board meeting at which a decision was made not to renew the contract of the home economics teacher, these boys came forward to defend her. As they were cross-examined, they acknowledged that they had taken her out on dates. That was that. Her contract was not renewed. Boys were no longer allowed to enroll in home economics class. And, so far, as I know, food at the Throckmorton schools was not tainted again.

Of course, the high school girls could generally match the high school boys in their antics. After the school purchased trampolines to place on the stage of Rice Auditorium, one group of girls quickly grew weary of performing the standard jumps and flips they learned from the physical education teacher and wife of the superintendent, Sue Stilley. At the back of the stage on which the trampolines resided, two steep stairways climbed to storage rooms at upstage right and left. The entryway to the storage room door was above even the curtain line at the front of the stage of Rice Auditorium. These girls noticed the potential of the entryway to the storage room as a launchpad for a cannonball plunge down onto the trampoline. This was from some thirty feet in the air! As one might imagine, the first time Sue Stilley caught these girls in the act of plummeting to what she was sure must be their serious injury or death, she took immediate action.

Even in a small, rural school, I saw a lot of students over a nearly forty-year career. If the average enrollment for all four years of students was one hundred or so, I suppose I knew or taught approximately one thousand students. How, then, could I hope to name them all? But just as the anecdotes come to mind so, too, do a sea of faces and grade book after grade book full of names. With the students from my first ten or fifteen years of teaching, I can place them in their particular year of graduation. The further the years progress, of course, the greater challenge it becomes. Then I refer to my yearbooks. In the 1962 yearbook I see so many faces, full of hope, smiling back at me: Caryn Clark, Jenny Liles, Elaine Bundy, Sarah Fowler, Valene Shaw, Pete Kitch, Kent Scrogum, Betty Crawford, Larry Cribbs, Billy Kay, Jack McWhorter, Toby Taylor, Berry Jennings, and Billy Nelson. What a lot of couples there were in this class: the bliss of romance, the misunderstandings and hurt feelings, the reconciliations, and, of course, the friendships. In 1963 the students I taught in fifth grade were now in high school, and I got to enjoy them all over again. And I recall students for a variety of reasons. Sharon London's mother made the best treats to sell at the concession stands during ball games. Mary Sanders and Ricky Johnson were skilled and reliable journalists for the school newspaper, *The Kennel*. Beth Manuel faithfully pursued her music studies and now equally faithfully plays the piano for services at the Methodist churches in Elbert and Throckmorton. Kay Nelson and Jimmy Rogers were faithful, too—to each other: they married and began a long and happy life together. In the 1964 yearbook I note a number of students who have made us proud in their professional lives: Larry Lilly, Jimmy Meng, Mike Cogburn, Tommy Gentry, Gerald Hilly, and Roy Bailes. I remember Anne Cooper, Kandy Cornelius, Nan Gentry, and Linda Karl for their delightful sense of humor; they always found fun and something to laugh about in class. Connis Daws, in contrast, always kept a poker face, even when he was guilty of this or that. One large class with many memorable students included, among the girls: Kay Condron, Linda Cribbs, Margaret and Marilyn Davis, Julie Hardy, Darlene Harrington, Diane Hitch, Addie Beth Craft, Karen Nichols, Lynda Pankey, and Judy Peacock. There were twins in that class as well: Danny and Diane Smith. These students were talented in academics—many in *Who's Who*—and athletics. I had to keep a close eye on senior boys through the years so they didn't put the poor freshmen through too much grief. In spite of any temporary memory lapses in their senior year on what it had been like to be a freshman, John Keeter, Matt Davis, Bruce Richardson, Larry Manuel, Johnny Allen, Gary Boland, Matt Chick, Jay Gober, Vannie Johnson, Stanny Liles, George London, and Bob McWhorter were all great fellows. In later years I remember an unfortunate practice that began in which senior boys would twist their senior ring so that the stone side faced down and then pop an unsuspecting "frosh" on his head. One day I noted that one of the senior boys in my class had taken off his ring during typing class and set it on his desk. I knew that he had been a frequent and unrepentant "ring popper," so while he typed, I discreetly slipped his ring on my finger (it was too big), held it steady, and gave him a slight pop on his head. He let out a cry and looked at me in surprise.

"Why did you do that, Mrs. Cypert?"

"It didn't feel good, did it?" I asked, quite seriously.

"No, it didn't. In fact, it kinda hurt."

"Imagine how much more it hurts when you pop the freshmen boys on the head," I replied.

"OK, OK," he said. "I get it."

And I never heard of, or saw, him bothering the freshman boys again.

Those senior rings could be dangerous in a variety of ways. On one occasion Walter and one of the coaches walked into the gym to see one of the senior boys, hanging by his arm, from the basketball hoop. It seems he and some of his classmates had been horsing around with a basketball and he had decided to go in for a layup in his street clothes, street shoes, and without removing his senior ring. In a bit of showmanship, he decided to make the layup a slam dunk, and somehow the ring caught on one of the metal hooks of the hoop that held the net. Because of Walter and the coach's timely appearance and the speedy acquisition of a ladder to extricate the student, the worst he suffered was a finger pulled out of joint. The experience served as a cautionary tale for students in the years to come.

Recalling the twins Danny and Diane Smith reminds me of some of the other twins we had in school over the years: Harry and Dick Hibbitts, Kay and Ray Ingram, Eddie and Freddie Barrington, Rita and Freda Haile, and Haylee and Heidi Briles. J. W. and Maureen Hibbitts were our neighbors up the hill, so when they and their first son, Tommy, welcomed the twins, they decided to have a Tom, Dick, and Harry. Of course, there were other families with several siblings. I remember, in particular, Johnny, Mike, and Tommy Martin, as well as the children of our doctor at the time, Sam, Mike, Bill, and daughter Lettie Nacol. I also remember quite well the students from and around the time of my sons' graduating classes of 1973 and 1978, having known them from six years old when they and my sons entered school. A series of birthday parties, field trips, and other school activities make these students easy to recall.

In my last half-decade of teaching, the 1980s, I seemed to have nearly as much fun as my first decade. Of course, now children, even grandchildren, of my former students were regularly entering my classroom, whereas when I started, it was only their younger brothers and sisters. In accounting class I was puzzled as to why Macalee Smith, who had seemed to have no problem in typing class, was inattentive. I would call on her to answer a question, and she would not answer. I went on to the next student. Finally, after giving her a third opportunity to answer a question, I walked over behind her and touched her on her shoulder. She nearly jumped out of her chair. The students chuckled and told me that Macalee tended to take her hearing aid out of her ear or turn it off during class. After that, every day when she would enter the classroom, I would look her squarely in the eyes and say, "Macalee, do you have it on?" She would laugh and say, "Yes, ma'am!"

One study hall I was in charge of was scheduled such that the two students had little or no homework to do, so I brought in Scrabble and other word games to keep them engaged—and working on their vocabulary at least. Cousins Jimmy Bruton and J. D. Bruton turned into great competitors for that hour. J. J. and Lori Cooper, who were sisters and cheerleaders, showed leadership skills by working with the principal and other cheerleaders to address the kinds of issues that many student groups face. And little did I know that when Charlotte Briles was enrolled in business subjects that I would be speaking with her on a regular basis in the future for my medical care, as she became the administrative assistant and business manager of the Throckmorton Clinic. I was equally curious about the future plans of the children of my colleagues and former colleagues, like Janet Boyd, who, taking after both her parents, completed her work quickly and accurately; or Mark Neely, who, like his parents, would go into education and, like his father, knew how to tell a good joke or story; Don Davis would saunter into my classroom with a package of chewing gum and offer me a slice, which I always refused and added that I did not want to see him chewing it either. There are so many sweet students whose names and faces grace my memories: Carla Cook, Cindy Cook, Tracie Davis, Tammie Davis, Marianne Morrison, Mitzi Priddy, Jon Hooper, Cindy Manual, and Rhonda Thornton. Of course having Tot Richards' daughters, Debbie, Darla, and Donna, in class in the 1970s and '80s brought back memories of Tot in school, as when the girls described how he would punish them: assigning push-ups, nonstop if necessary, to prevent their arguing with him. In 1982 Glenn Boyd, Fred Thorpe, and siblings Ken and Konnie Koonsman showed up on the scene. Whenever I asked a question requiring an affirmative answer, Ken would always respond, "Thaaaat's riiiiiiight," his voice rising higher on the second word; when I began responding to him in kind, he had a fit of giggles. The Hagle girls were always gracious about helping to get things done. In 1984 we discovered what a beautiful voice Karlyn Hibbitts had, what a talent Oby Ray Broyles had in hair design, and what a happy disposition Jimmy Goode always had with a smile to match. John Riley, always a good student, displayed a natural aptitude for economics. And Sammy Cook, the little stinker, could not sneeze without violating my classroom ban on foul language, as I previously reported, resulting in my sitting on the floor with the soap when he crawled under his desk to escape. I waited and he waited and at last came out to take his medicine. Some of these students settled in Throckmorton and married a high school sweetheart, as was the case with Diane Selfe and Charlie Balthrop. Some of the students came from abroad, as did Thuen Hoang and Minh Hoang from Vietnam, learning English from television as quickly as from their classmates. In 1986 Donnell Brown, as a sophomore, requested and received special permission to take typing, which was limited to juniors. Knowing of my retirement, he wanted to take typing from the person who had taught his two sisters and brother. When Dow Latham signed up for typing, his mother, Valene, a former student and fellow teacher, said, "Mrs. Cypert, his other teachers have reported he can be a little restless." "Don't worry," I replied. "He will be too busy to even think about leaving his seat." And so he was. And like so many other former students, Aimee Liles Hale, from whom I often get a hug at church on Sundays, runs her own business, the old Liles-Boyd Abstracting and Insurance Company, where I got my start so many years ago from her great-grandfather.

CHAPTER SIX

With Whom I Taught

I began my teaching career in August of 1947. That fall term, there were approximately 127 students enrolled in the high school, which employed a total of ten faculty members. Class size was generally around twenty-five. The eight elementary school classes, which met in the basement, had approximately one teacher for each class. The high school faculty included Mr. Gregory (English, also the local Presbyterian minister, who had difficulties keeping his students from slipping out the window to visit the candy store across the street), Mrs. Robinett (math), Mr. Woods (science and principal), Mr. Little (history, who also served as coach), Mrs. Sam Massey (home economics), Mr. Steele (vocational agriculture), Mr. Ward (band director), Mrs. Jonel Condron (librarian and English teacher), and Mr. Powers (the superintendent, who taught chemistry). I have always thought it a good idea for administrators to teach at least one class to remind them of the challenges and joys that their faculty members face.

While it was important to get to know to my faculty colleagues, I learned quite early the professional value of forming a friendship with the employees who knew the most of what went on at the school: the custodians. At that time Throckmorton schools were fortunate to have three loyal and dedicated employees who maintained the physical plant: Mr. T. K. (Truman) Ball, Mr. Joe Daws, and Mr. C. T. Kelley. Mr. Ball was in charge of the gymnasium (Rice Auditorium), ensuring that its hardwood floors stayed in pristine condition and protecting them from any students (or faculty) who might stray onto the floor with street shoes. Mr. Daws maintained the school building and, like Mr. Ball, was up each day in the winter, as early as three-thirty a.m., to ensure enough coal had been shoveled into the furnace so that the building was warm when school began at eight a.m. Mr. Kelley was hired after the construction of the vocational agriculture building to provide support to Mr. Daws. In the afternoon, during my conference period, Mr. Daws would stop by my room to sweep, empty the trash, and share the news from around the school that I needed to know—which might include information from the minutes of the school board, which always seemed to have been left out in plain view when he was cleaning the administrative offices. Mr. Ball, Mr. Daws, and Mr. Kelley had long careers at the Throckmorton School and were much beloved.

One of the many pleasures of teaching in my hometown was welcoming my former students, who, after attending college, returned to Throckmorton, as I did, to teach. One of the first, during my teaching career, was James Beach, who in 1961 completed my teaching duties for me the year I gave birth to Rick. In 1962 Tommy Boyd was hired to coach, and in 1963 Bob Neely joined the faculty as science teacher. Both were favorites of mine. I got a kick out of watching Bob interact with his students, some of whom, like he as a high school student, did not like to be corrected. We all recall as teachers pretty quickly what we were like as students when we see some bright young person ready to challenge us or our subjects or school rules. In my case I was frequently reminded of what a "talker" I had been as a student and how amused many of my former teachers must have been at the thought of my working with a bunch of other chatty students. Although he did not teach in Throckmorton, as his father had, Glenn Boyd, one of my former students, did teach one year. I would have loved to have been present on his first day of teaching. I always got a kick out of Glenn, but I could only imagine his reaction to student behavior now as a teacher. Meanwhile, more former graduates of Throckmorton High School would join our faculty: in the 1960s Billy Don Davis, Don Sims, Sue Beach, and in the 1970s George London, Charles and Sharon (Curtis) Gober, Barbara (Ash) Walker, Nel Rey (Daws) Coker, Donniece (Johnson) Neely, Johnny

Martin, Mike and Joy (Estridge) Cogburn, and in the 1980s Katrina (Cook) Briles and Christine (McCarty) Timmons.

This was no new tradition. Many Throckmorton teachers in years past were also graduates, including Mrs. Lorena (Bachman) Cochran, Mrs. Florence (Bachman) Robinett, Beulah Lou (Lee) Grable, Beth (Lee) Craft, Glennie (Boyd) Nelson, and Dorothy (Martin) Lilly. These teachers came and stayed and, in the case of the elementary school, my husband, the principal, enjoyed over a decade of a consistent, unchanging faculty. Although not all of these teachers graduated from Throckmorton, they did commit their lives and many years of service to the school: Laverne Mc-Carson (first grade), Billy Condron (second), Beulah Lou Grable (third), Glennie Nelson (fourth), Nadine Hurley (fifth), Dorothy Lilly (sixth), Sue (Beach) Sims (seventh), and Don Sims (eighth). And the tradition of hiring our graduates as teachers continues.

Of course, teachers who did not graduate from Throckmorton joined our faculty as well and became dear friends. In 1965 the school hired Linda (Ball) Perry as girl's coach and economics teacher. In later years she would teach junior high, including Texas history, which my younger son counts among his favorite subjects from school. Linda had traveled to Mexico and had also brought back coins as prizes for students who scored well on exams. She maintained an activity-based classroom where students were learning by doing, as, for example, when they made salt, flour, and paste topographical maps of the state or built miniature replicas of the Alamo out of sugar cubes. Her knowledge of the southern part of our county, down by the Clear Fork of the Brazos River, meant memorable trips for her students each spring to the Watt Matthews Ranch. And, as I earlier mentioned, Linda was skilled in shorthand, which meant she and I could write notes back and forth to one another during less-than-scintillating moments of school meetings or professional development days when experts from the regional education offices visited the rural schools to conduct workshops.

As a faculty we were a close-knit group, socializing as well as working together. After each home football game, the teachers would get together to discuss the game and visit. At the end of each school year we met at a park or ranch for a picnic and cookout. Each Christmas, Mrs. Barney (Louise Russell) Davis, who had previously taught home economics at our school and whose children had been our students, hosted a holiday bridge party. The faculty members who loved to play bridge got together more than once a year, however. We had regular get-togethers through the year. Whoever hosted the party also provided coffee and dessert. Whenever Walter and I hosted, I often asked my mother, a wonderful baker, to prepare a cake. On one occasion in March, however, I made the cake. Because we were getting together right before Saint Patrick's Day, I decided to modify the red velvet cake, a real crowd-pleaser that my mother often made, by adding green, rather than red, food coloring.

One of my colleagues and former students, Billy Don Davis, upon walking in the door, grinned and called out, "What did your mother prepare for us this evening?"

I looked sternly at him as I responded.

"I will have you know, Billy Don, that I prepared tonight's dessert!"

And everyone praised the green velvet cake in honor of Saint Patrick. Later, however, Walter and I would discover, much to my dismay, that the green food coloring was indigestible, a fact shared with no one outside of our family until now. Creative bakers, beware!

During the years I taught high school, all was not sweetness and light. Around the middle of one year the superintendent and principal called all the teachers together for a faculty meeting. The superintendent, deadly serious, began the meeting by urging all teachers to do a better job of monitoring the hallways between classes.

"There is too much petting going on in the halls," he said. "You need to do a better job of correcting students who engage in public displays of affection."

This certainly caught my attention. I had corrected students for such behavior and for sitting on the front steps of the school instead of reporting to class. Each time they returned from their visits to the principal's office, seemingly unchastened—perhaps even amused by the experience. The most recent time I had done so, the students I sent informed me that the principal would not do anything.

Other teachers knew this to be so. I looked around, but my colleagues remained silent. I did not. I raised my hand and spoke my mind.

"In this case it does not seem to do much good to send students to the principal's office, as the students report that nothing is done."

That night, my husband, who had been present at the meeting, told me that I should be ready to be contacted the next day. "You really infuriated the principal," he said.

And, sure enough, the next day the principal sent word that he wanted to see me in the superintendent's office.

After alerting me in no uncertain terms that he did not appreciate teachers conveying the attitude, so publicly in a faculty meeting, that he did not discipline students, the principal asked, "Is there anything else that I need to say?"

The superintendent paused, looked first at me and then at the principal, before saying, "Well, I actually agree with Minta about this discipline issue. Minta, you are excused."

After many years in a school building constructed in 1912, the elementary teachers and students moved into a new building constructed in 1955. Even though students today must find it quaint, in 1955 the building was state-of-the-art: a combined cafeteria, tile floor marked for basketball and four hoops that could be raised or lowered for practice, and a stage at one end with draw curtain and footlights (we called it the cafetorium); terrazzo floors; main bathrooms with showers; utility rooms between primary-grades classrooms and in-class bathrooms for the primary-grade classrooms as well; a wall of windows for each room, later partially occupied by swamp coolers; a library; a book room; a principal's office with intercom system; and large playgrounds on either side of the school. Because I was teaching fifth grade that year, I got to move to the new building and enjoy the luxury but would return to the old building the following year.

A decade later, in 1966, it was the high school's turn. The old building was imploded, and a new space-age building of white brick with modern lines was constructed in front of the location of the old high school, lined up alongside the elementary school. As with the elementary school building, which my husband, Walter; the superintendent; school board members; and architects had carefully designed, the new high school was a group effort as well. Jonel Condron, the librarian, designed the layout of the library in the center of the building; Mrs. Milton Fox helped design the home economics room with three kitchen stations, a sewing area, a living room area for practice in entertaining, and a classroom area. Walter and I were so impressed with the products purchased for the facility that when it was time to bring in new appliances, we purchased one of the retractable stove and double oven (on top) sets from the school. And I had a say in how the business subjects classroom would be designed. I searched for and found student desks both with modesty panels and attached right-angle typewriter tables, so they were suitable for shorthand, bookkeeping, and typing classes. Off the main classroom, I incorporated a storage closet and three small, soundproof practice rooms so that students could come in when other classes were in progress and practice typing, Dictaphone, shorthand, and bookkeeping skills. It was a wonderful teaching space, and I felt fortunate to have been able to help design it.

With the new building came new teachers: Darren and Geneva Rodgers (math and English) and Linda Perry (as I mentioned). In 1966 the yearbook was dedicated to the student body, and we were joined by Royce Priddy as the vocational agriculture teacher and Milton Fox as the band director. Some of us that year decided to meet in the gym to play volleyball and use the exercise equipment during our free period. In 1968 Coach Tommy Boyd became High School Principal Tommy Boyd. After designing the library for our new high school, Jonel Condron enjoyed it only for a short period of time as an exciting job opportunity took her to the library at North Texas State University, and in 1968 we welcomed Linda Wells as the new high school librarian. For many years Mrs. Claude (Maureen) Keeter served as the elementary school librarian, who became the yearbook dedicatee in 1978. In 1968 the yearbook was dedicated to Mrs. Pearl Falls, who had served as piano teacher for many years and as accompanist for graduation ceremonies and assembly programs, among many other school events. Another notable alumna, Marilois Kirksey, was the dedicatee of the yearbook in 1969 for her many years of missionary work in Brazil. In 1967 Mrs. Charlie (Bonnie) Morris joined our faculty as home economics teacher, and Mr. Grogan served as the band director. Mr. Tony served as band director in 1970—band directors in small schools seem to move on, as coaches sometimes do, rather quickly.

Regional, national, and world events often coincided with our school days. So when one of our former students, Bob Lilly, named to the Pro Football Hall of Fame, retired as a defensive tackle for the Dallas Cowboys, the yearbook was dedicated to him in 1974, along with other honors since. As the country celebrated its bicentennial in 1976, the Junior-Senior Banquet theme was "Spirit of '76," and, as mentioned earlier, new teachers/former students, "patriotic" to their school, joined our ranks: Charles and Sharon (Curtis) Gober, Joy (Estridge) Cogburn, and Nel Rey (Daws) Coker.

Along with joyful times we also mourned as a school and community. Although many of my former students and colleagues have died, the deaths that occurred while these students and teachers were still directly a part of our community stand out in my memory. In 1960 Emma Jo (Holcomb) Cogburn, one of our elementary school teachers, died unexpectedly while undergoing routine surgery, a great loss to all of us. In 1962 Kathy Larson died from burns received at her home. In 1974 our much beloved second-grade teacher, Billy (Sawyer) Condron, died after a long battle with cancer. The loss was equally great even when students or faculty had graduated or recently retired. A few years after her retirement in 1972, Mrs. Bonnie Morris (home economics) died in a car wreck with her husband, Charlie, while returning from visiting their son in college at Lubbock. In 1977 Toby Payne, who had just graduated, died after coming in contact with a live electrical wire while working. The year after her retirement as school librarian, Linda Wells died in a car wreck with her husband, Doyle, on a return trip from Colorado. Car wrecks also claimed the lives of Jan Milligan and David Dunlap. While every death of a former or current student, teacher, administrator, or staff member receives focused community attention, these, because of circumstances, were particularly poignant.

* * *

As I have mentioned, in a small school and community, we knew each other pretty well. Doors were left unlocked, and, as with a former neighbor who used to announce, "Coming in," as she walked in our front door without ringing the bell or knocking, privacy was not considered an issue. Such was the case one morning when I was changing clothes. I had walked into the kitchen, where our combination washer/dryer was located, to retrieve an item of clothing. My former student, now colleague, Coach George London, had stopped by to ask Walter something and walked into the house, without knocking, and into the kitchen, right as I entered the kitchen from the other door in only my undergarments.

"George," I exclaimed and ducked back into the other room.

"Mrs. Cypert," he responded (rather than his usual "Minta Sue").

"I am sorry," he called out as he headed into the other room where Walter was now waiting. "Don't worry, though, my mom walks around the house in her underwear, too."

After George left and when Walter stopped laughing, later on, he reassured me not to worry.

"Haven't you noticed that George always wears his wildest-colored underwear on the day that he wears his thin, white coaching pants? I don't think he worries much about underwear."

Walter and I enjoyed the coaches with whom we worked. But coaches and teachers, of course, often have a different perspective. Such was the case earlier in my career, when one day Jimmy Matthews and Jean Paul Cornelius came strolling into my afternoon class, giggling.

"Hello, Mrs. Cypert. How are you?" Jimmy called out.

"Hello, Jimmy," I responded and knew immediately something was amiss. Although a sweet boy, Jimmy Matthews was an unlikely candidate to initiate conversation or provide a greeting. As I walked around the room and passed near Jimmy's and Jean Paul's desks, I could tell that they had been drinking alcohol during the lunchtime break. I asked the boys to accompany me to the principal's office, reported them, and returned to class. The principal, Ray Stark, conferred with Mr. Powers, the superintendent, who conferred with the basketball coach, Morris Mercer—Jimmy and Jean

Paul were wonderful basketball players. After class when I met with the superintendent, principal, and coach; Mr. Powers began the meeting.

"Ah, well, Mrs. Cypert, I do not think we can be sure that these boys were drinking."

"I didn't smell anything on them," Coach Mercer helpfully supplied.

Mr. Powers frowned slightly and then continued.

"Is it, uh, possible, that they could have eaten yeast?"

"I suppose many things are possible," I replied, "but those boys had been drinking."

The boys were not disciplined, so when they returned to my class during an off period to make up their work, I refused to let them until they convinced me that I had not been imagining things. They chuckled and admitted that they had found a bottle of liquor and imbibed a bit but promised that they would not return to my class in such a state in the future. I then allowed them to make up their work.

The following week, Coach Mercer called the basketball team together, having heard that some of the players had been smoking cigarettes.

"Those of you who have been smoking can just turn in your uniforms," Mercer barked. "And I know who you are. I can smell it on you."

This speech, of course, traveled around the school, so when I next saw Morris, I smiled and said, "Well, Morris, it seems that although some people cannot smell alcohol, their nose is fine-tuned to pick up tobacco."

Morris turned red and said, "Now, Minta Sue, I don't want to hear another word."

And he didn't—from me—but I had made my point. And the basketball players' uniforms were returned to them, in time for the next game.

Where does one stop when the floodgates of memories open? Can one find room for one more name? Who has one forgotten? So many. Too many. In 1977 the yearbook was dedicated to Billy Shankles, another local graduate, who served as school custodian for many years. Another graduate who worked as custodian was Johnny Messenger. In the 1980s Bobby Bundy, another graduate and former student, began work on the building and grounds crew at the school. Since my retirement, Ray and Gayle (Shankles) Fowler began working at the school as well, just as Ray's mother and Gayle's father had: Ray on building and grounds and Gayle working with the music and arts programs. Our school has been fortunate to have many dedicated staff members to work at the school. I previously mentioned Truman Ball and Joe Daws, who maintained our physical plant along with Mr. C. T. Kelly. Beginning in 1949, Mrs. and Mrs. Frank Stroud worked for many years in the school cafeteria, along with Dona Taylor and Esmer Conner. In 1958 Lank (Langston Clifford) Millican served as the head of the cafeteria, followed by Mrs. Faye Nichols in 1963. That same year Mrs. Brown began working at the cafeteria, and she was joined by Mrs. Bundy, Mrs. Smith, and Mrs. Ingram in 1965. When Faye Nichols retired, Mrs. Billy Ray (Pat) Fowler assumed the position and later Vonnie Jones. Many locals have also served as bus drivers for the school, for what used to be an extensive route through the country, including Frank Stroud, Merle Lawson, Buddy Thompson, Ray Barr, Woody Timms, Bernard Gilmore, Cork Burkhalter, Audie Herod, Mr. Cook, A. D. Rogers, Huston Hare, Johnny Kimbrell, Mont Nash, Wes Hulcy, and Van Moses.

For many years Florence Huston was a fixture in the tax office, housed at that time in the high school. Ruby Dunlap later assumed this position. Across the hall, Edmee Rae (E. D.) Johnson, my high school classmate and friend, served as the school and superintendent's secretary for many years until her retirement. Debbie (Rogers) Timmons, another graduate, has since served in that position. Debbie (Self) Hargrove serves in the elementary school office. Gloria Barrett joined the school staff in the 1980s as the high school principal's secretary and also became a good friend.

Staffing changes began occurring more quickly in the late 1970s and 1980s as longtime faculty and staff began retiring. A new coach, Tommy Thompson, and science teacher, Bill Ed Crowley (brother to librarian and teacher Linda Wells and Judy Stewart), joined the faculty. The 1981 yearbook was dedicated to Mr. and Mrs. Hurley (superintendent and fifth-grade teacher), Dorothy Lilly (sixth grade), and Tommy Boyd (high school principal and coach), who all retired in 1980. And after he retired in 1981, the 1982 yearbook was dedicated to Walter. A new superintendent, Derrith Welch; a new elementary principal, Gerald Butler; and new coaches, Buddy Husted and Clio Johnson, promised to bring new changes to the school.

Bill Woods became the new high school principal. The theme of the 1983 Junior-Senior Banquet, "Over the Rainbow," seemed particularly apt, as many longed for happier times: many of the "new" changes brought about disappointment, frustration, and some broken friendships.

In 1987 Laverne (Manuel) McCarson, the first-grade teacher of my younger son (who graduated in 1978), retired, and the yearbook was dedicated to her. In 1986 I retired (as I shall detail later), and in 1987 the yearbook was dedicated to the football fans and to Edmee Rae (E. D.) Johnson, the school secretary, for her twenty-nine years of service. In 1987 Ward Cooksey became the new superintendent; Mr. Johnson was named as principal; Gus Dormier served as head coach along with his colleagues Scott Hogue and Coach Glass. Both Dormier and Hogue would later serve in administrative positions at the school. Other former students, Nancy (Redwine) Bachman and Diane (Self) Balthrop, would later join the elementary school faculty.

And that's about it. There is not much more to my official affiliation with the Throckmorton school system. After I retired, I continued to substitute regularly for about twenty years, and after that, the school continued to allow me to register as a substitute each year. But aside from those faculty and staff who are still there, who were there, when I retired, now precious few, I do not know the new personalities that enliven the halls. I do not know the students, except by name, as in the many cases of grandchildren and great-grandchildren of my former students. And that is as it must be. The next chapter in the history of Throckmorton and of the Throckmorton schools is to be written by someone else, who may or may not be a hometown girl or hometown boy. But I still have a little left to say. And that begins on the next page.

CHAPTER SEVEN

Still a Hometown Girl

I am sitting on a rock overlooking the Aegean Sea, surrounded by students who are not my own—they are my son's. He is conversing with them about the history of the place and the Greek temple behind us that they have just examined. He is standing in front of us, his back to the sea, asking the students questions and responding to them. I follow a little bit of the conversation, but I am mainly focused on how near he is to the cliff, but neither he nor his students seem the least bit concerned. They are having fun. I have accompanied this group on a study-abroad course to Greece in order to see a place where my son has spent his sabbaticals and many summers, and to watch him teach.

That is May. In September of another year I am in a high school football stadium with my older son, watching his son, my grandson, play football. A referee makes a bad call; my son calls out. The referee misses a call; I call out. A woman turns around in her seat and observes to my son, "I guess we know where you come by it." My son chuckles about this comment for days and calls me while on one of his business trips to remind me of it. When either of my boys gets too agitated, I try to calm them down. But when do we, as parents, stop trying to protect our children, whether on a cliff in Greece or a football stadium in Texas? Never, I guess.

After many happy years of teaching, my husband, Walter, retired in 1981. Because of his three years of service in the Navy, he had additional years to apply to his retirement. For my retirement I would need to teach at least three more years, but in 1982 Walter experienced his first heart attack and had no insurance to cover him, so I continued teaching until 1986, when the teacher retirement system of Texas set up insurance for all retired teachers. In 1986 Walter had open-heart surgery, so, at the end of the year, I decided I should retire, but I cried all summer about the decision. That year Walter, Rick, and I took a trip to Jamaica so I could be out of town when school started, climbing a river waterfall rather than walking up and down the rows of desks, ensuring that the students' hands were on the home keys and their eyes were on the wall chart as I called out letters.

Even though retiring from teaching, at age sixty-three, was difficult, I certainly could not complain about recognition. In addition to seeing former students at homecoming and every day in my hometown, I had been elected as Coming-Home Queen in 1976, had been recognized as the outstanding teacher for the year in 1984–85, and was selected as the outstanding ex-student from Throckmorton High School in 2002.

And I had my family. My older son, Chuck, graduated from North Texas State University and then completed his master's degree at Saint Thomas University in Houston. Like Walter and me, he studied business. Rick graduated from McMurry College and then completed his master's degree at Iowa State University. He taught high school for a couple of years and then returned to graduate school, this time at Texas Christian University, where he completed his doctorate in English. Over the years Chuck has lived and worked in business in Houston and the Dallas area, as well as up north (North Dakota and Michigan) for a time. In 1987 Rick moved to Lincoln, where he teaches at Nebraska Wesleyan University.

I am proud of my sons, but I am also a proud grandmother. Chuck's son, Steven, loves all sports. He plays soccer and football. All through high school, he kept me updated on his sporting events and academic progress, and Chuck regularly brought me to Plano to watch Steve's sporting events. Now Steve has enrolled at Texas Tech University in order to pursue his future.

Now retired for twenty-five years and, like many seniors, fortunate to live on relatively healthy, I have found new ways to spend my time. For the first fifteen years or so I continued to substitute at the school. While he was alive, Walter and I traveled a good bit with Rick, often flying to various locations to meet up with him after he would complete a seminar. I remained active in my church women's group and other church activities, attended a quilting group and made some quilts of my own, and participated in community efforts, such as the historical society's county history book and planning for various Veterans' Day events. How do these various activities and events add up to a life? That, I suppose, is why I set out, with my son, to write this book: to tell a story and, in the process, figure out what it means.

✳ ✳ ✳

What does it mean to be a "hometown girl"? I had not really thought about it consciously, I guess, until talking with my younger son. He teaches rhetorical theory, among other subjects, at a liberal arts college and wants to claim that two Greek terms, *ethos* (identity) and *topos* (place) have become intertwined in my case. I suppose that might be true. I was born in Throckmorton, grew up in Throckmorton, spent my working career in Throckmorton, and have retired in Throckmorton. I expect to die and be buried in Throckmorton as well. Except for my years in college in nearby Abilene, a few summers working on my master's degree in Denton, and some wonderful vacations, I have not left Throckmorton for very long periods of time. In this age of mobility and migration, that might be a little unusual, but probably not so much for many people of my generation.

In part, I guess I *have* tied my identity to this place. For many years I was responsible for registering returning students at the school homecoming event, and I still keep a notebook in which I register the addresses of our alumni and, sadly, note which ones have died in the intervening years. Along with many others, I served on a committee to put together a history of Throckmorton County that was published in a large volume and which serves to jog my memory. At church I make note of who is visiting and who is connected with whom. For many years I made Monday morning telephone calls to friends who attended other churches in order to write down a list of their visitors with which to assemble a visitors-in-town column for the local newspaper. When I have the chance, I like to ride around the town, noting where people are living, who is new in town, and where homes are being built. The countryside around town, likewise, offers a chance to observe how the crops are faring in wet and in dry years, where cattle are being pastured, the raising of new barns or the digging of new tanks (stock ponds), and where new oil exploration is taking place or new pumps have been installed. Do I find my identity in this land—mesquite tree, cactus, rocky soil, and far-stretching horizon—has the land made me who I am? I guess it has made me see its beauty in its sparseness. I can pick out details on this prairie and farmland as easily as I observed a letter of a mistyped key on the stark white paper turned in by my typing students so long ago. If you look closely, the knarred branch of a tree on the side of the road might be as graceful as the well-executed curl of one of Gregg's semiscript symbols in shorthand.

And I know the land by knowing how much of it there is. All those years ago at the County Agriculture Extension office, I rolled a small instrument across aerial photographs of this county, determining tracts of land, and later as an abstractor, noting who owned which land, how much land. And I know this land by knowing to whom it belongs. This place is also populated by people, after all: relatives, classmates, and neighbors of mine, though fewer, now represented by children and grandchildren and, of course, my students from days gone by.

It is an activity of senior citizens, of older people, of old people: counting and recounting. Counting the number of people who have moved to town, who have moved away (and to where), and who have died. Recounting stories of days gone by. Sometimes younger people join in on this activity and the oral tradition is carried forward. Long before, and even after, our county history book was published, I remember walking down the hill to the home of our next-door neighbor and good friend Ollie Condron to ask about this or that person and how he or she was connected to other families in town. Ollie was a wealth of information about the whole county. She had grown up on Hog Creek, out toward Elbert, but was as likely to launch into a story about a family in Woodson in the southern part of the county as she was to mention someone from Elbert, closer to her own stompin' grounds. Ollie was a great example of a life well lived, of someone who knew how to keep busy and tend to her own knitting. Long after her husband C. C. ("Monk") died, and shortly after the death of another neighbor, Maureen Hibbitt's husband, J. W., Ollie worked out a deal with Maureen in which Maureen bought the groceries and Ollie cooked. Lunch and dinnertime found these two engaged in lively conversation, if not a difference of opinion, about this or that. On one occasion, Ollie had not only Maureen but another friend, Pearl Bryant, in attendance, and Maureen and Pearl were exchanging stories about their aches and pains.

"Well, Pearl, you don't look as though you feel well now," Maureen opined.

"Oh, I don't," Pearl acknowledged. "I was sick as could be last night throwing up."

"What caused that?" Ollie asked.

"You know, I don't know," Pearl replied. "I went to bed early after taking some Doan's Pills that Steve [her late husband] always used when he had a backache."

"Good Lord, Pearl," Ollie interjected. "Steve has been dead twenty years. You should have thrown out those pills."

"Yes," Pearl said, the realization dawning upon her. "That must have been what made me sick."

Ever sharp and attentive to those things needing done, Ollie continued to mow her own lawn, long after most senior citizens would think to do so. She would be up early summer mornings, whistling a church hymn as she hung out her laundry. Her repertoire ran the breadth and length of the Cokesbury hymnal, and beyond. "Sweet Hour of Prayer" might well be followed by the livelier "There's within My Heart a Melody" and topped off by one that she lived, "Work for the Night Is Coming." Even in her house, her hands were busy: ironing, snapping beans, cracking pecans brought to her from the courthouse square. She attended Sunday School (the "Mary Martha Class") and the Ladies' Missionary Society with my mother. Each week the Sunday School class signed cards for many people, young and old, both in our church and other churches, to commemorate or acknowledge the loss of a loved one, an illness, the joy of a wedding, the birth of a baby, or the celebration of a birthday. She also attended funerals, just about every funeral that occurred. Sometimes these funerals were for former residents, long since moved away from Throckmorton, and so elderly that fewer and fewer people remembered them. But Ollie did. Even if she did not know the person, she attended the funeral because, as she would say, "Everyone deserves at least one person at their funeral." While Ollie might not have been the sole congregant at any funeral, there were occasions when she was one of the very few.

So it is a habit to cultivate: the ritual of meaningful activity, of getting something done. Certainly my mother did. As she grew older, she not only took care of my boys, but, as I have mentioned, she loved to cook. So she would bake wonderful cakes—red velvet, German chocolate, Italian cream, Milky Way bar—but, conscious of her weight, would put them in the freezer to have at the ready to take to a church luncheon or funeral dinner. When her freezer was full of cakes, she would drop by a neighbor's home with the gift, or later, when she could not drive, call the neighbor to stop by. Because what so often motivates us as humans is our need to connect with others, to be reminded of who they are and who we are.

✳ ✳ ✳

It is 1966 or 1968 or 1970 or all of the above and more, and I would like to leave the concession stand for just a moment during the halftime intermission of this homecoming game to peer down on the football field. A sea of Stetson and cowboy hats block my view. Throngs of people mill about as well, many crowding up at the concession stand window to make a purchase. Nonetheless, I can hear the marching band performing its routine and then the cries and loud applause as some of the twirlers light their batons and send fiery circles of flame into the sky, before catching them perfectly. Then, over the loudspeaker, the announcer welcomes the nominees for homecoming queen onto the field. Brand-new vehicles from Morris or, later, Burkhalter Chevrolet, shined to perfection, drive slowly around the edge of the field, the hood of each vehicle adorned with a lovely young woman holding a bouquet of flowers. With help from their escorts, each nominee gracefully dismounts from her mechanical steed and walks to the center of the field where the homecoming queen is named and crowned.

Meanwhile, in the concession stand, with a ridiculously large purple-and-gold spangled chrysanthemum corsage pinned to my lapel, I am helping the other sponsors and student workers serve up sandwiches, chili dogs, brownies, cake, giant sour pickles, lemon halves with peppermint sticks stuck in them, hot coffee, hot chocolate, Coca-Colas, and a variety of other goodies. It is a crazy, yet graceful, dance we do around each other in the small concession stand while chatting with our locals and being good hosts to the fans of the visiting team. Laughter and shouts ring out as old friends and neighbors, some having moved far away, recognize one another and reach out to shake hands.

Clearly, one of my favorite things to do, in this small town, is attending parties or school events at which I encounter former students who hug me and tell me how much I influenced and helped them in the classes I taught. Especially at homecoming, when so many of them return. I can now, released from concession stand duties, make my way slowly through the bleachers in the football stadium to my seat, buoyed up, nurtured by the affection of wave upon wave of former students who stand to greet and hug me. As I tell everyone, these moments are the "icing on the cake of teaching" for me. In their lives and being, in their happiness and success, and, yes, even their moments of sadness, I find my *ethos*, my identity, who I am. I am someone for these former students, especially those who have moved away, who is still here; someone who helps them reclaim and reconnect who they were and where they lived with that person they have become.

But I am not unique. So, too, are there many hometown girls and boys in Throckmorton and in every small town in this nation and around the world who have stayed in their small community and made a life, their interests and identity equally tied together with the waxing and waning fortunes of that place they call home.

I stand at the locked gate of a country cemetery in Fannin County, Texas. My son is balancing on the gate, one foot on the hinges outside the cemetery, the other stretching out to touch the inside hinge. With a wide swing of his left leg he is over the fence and inside the cemetery. He reaches over the gate to take the camera I have been holding and some flowers we have brought to place at the grave of Ellen Roxana Parmenter, my grandfather's younger sister, who came down with the measles on the trip from Illinois, as did her sister, Mary Alice. Unlike Mary Alice, however, Ellen did not recover, and on June 24, 1872, thirteen days after her ninth birthday, she died.

"Found it," my son calls out from the far end of the small cemetery. I watch him kneel and place the flowers at the grave and then start taking photographs.

Then he returns to the gate to ask for paper and pen.

"There's an inscription I want to work on," he says. "It's pretty faint."

While I go to the car, he walks over to take a photograph of Joseph Buchanan's grave.

"It's the same date," he says. "This is the Joe Buchanan who served on Sheriff Ragsdale's posse to capture the Dyer brothers."

He snaps more photos and moves from one grave to another. Then, paper and pen in hand, he goes to spend time at Ellen Parmenter's grave.

While he was unable to capture the inscription on another grave in the nearby Lindsey-Randolph cemetery, that of my grandfather's first wife, Ella Blackburn Parmenter, who died from tuberculosis at age twenty-nine, with the child Ellen's gravestone he succeeds. He returns to the gate and stands facing me, on the other side, and describes the stone, the photo of which I will later see. At the top is a carving of a dove in flight and below the following inscription (a stanza from Samuel Taylor Coleridge's 1832 revised "Epitaph on an Infant"), which he recites to me:

This lovely bud so young
so fair, called hence by

early doom. Just came
to show how sweet a
flower in Paradise would bloom.

We stand looking at each other for a moment, thinking about this child whose grave has not been visited in many years, who died a couple of months after arriving in a new place, far from the home she had known, the familiar present only in her mother, brother, and sister. Balancing again, my son steadies himself and then swings back over the gate. We are together again, on the same side. It is my first time to visit this place, this county where my grandfather spent his young adult years, where he met and married both his first and second wives, women whose families brought them here from somewhere else as well—hometowns far away. My son wants to find records, marriage certificates, and so on at the courthouse in nearby Bonham, and we do—evidence on paper of lives lived. By the time we leave the courthouse it is mid-afternoon, and clouds begin to roll in from the west. I am ready to head that direction, to return home.

W. E. Parmenter at his father's grave in Illinois (1948).

The old farmhouse where Minta, her mother, and her sister were born

Minta, her mother, Rena, and her sister Musetta.

At Buffalo Gap church camp. Dallas Perkins is third from left in the first row. Minta is second from right in the back row.

"THE GREYHOUND SPIRIT"

Part I—Self Realization

AN INQUIRING MIND

Reader .... Warren Criswell
Senior Graduate .... Dorothy Condron

PUBLIC HEALTH

Nurse .... Ray Laverne Fry
Crippled Boy .... Theron Oay Tharp
Health Girl .... Lorene Britt

RECREATION

Tennis Players .... John Lee Brown, Mary Ethel Tenney
Students Reading .... Barbara Nell Harrington, C. W. Howard
Football Boy .... Laurinton Keeler
Basketball Boy .... Bern Borger
Volleyball Girl .... Sally Lou Tharp
Doug. "End of a Perfect Year" .... J. W. Ash

Part II—Human Relationships

RESPECT FOR HUMANITY

Two Salvation Lasses .... Adrienne Smith, Billie Jean Grable
Tramp in Rags .... Ted Armstrong

COOPERATION AND FRIENDSHIP OF NATIONS

Uncle Sam .... Glenn McWhorter
Lily of France .... Oley Rhoades
John Bull .... John Copeland
Spain .... Elmore Ray Varner

FAMILY RELATIONSHIPS

Mother .... Blanche Denham
Father .... Max McCarson
Son .... Louie Glenn
Daughters .... Minta Sue Thompson, Billie Jean Scott

Part III—Economics Efficiency

Mother .... Lavenia Stroud
Father .... Douglas Tidrow
Son .... Sam Redwine
Daughter .... Sallie Sue Beaty

OCCUPATIONAL COOPERATION

Employee .... Derell Sorelle
Employer .... Dell Stout

VOCATIONAL GUIDANCE

Two Businessmen .... Marshall Thornton, Durwood Tucker

Part IV—Civic

LAW OBSERVANCE

Father .... D. O. Smith
Son .... Truman Stroud
Greyhound Spirit .... Addison Bachman

COMMUNITY PLANNING

Girl at Polls .... Mildred Ingram
Teacher .... George Hall Fair
Young Man .... Clark Burkhalter
Bad Citizen .... C. W. Carpenter
Southern Gentleman .... John Thomas Parrott
Greyhound Spirit .... Addison Bachman
Senior Graduate .... Graham Bachman

Part V—Presentations

Processional .... Mrs. James Putnam
Presentation of Awards .... A. S. Jackson, Principal
Presentation of Seniors .... Harry W. Rice, Superintendent
Presentation of Diplomas .... J. J. Keeler, President of School Board
Recessional .... Mrs. James P. Putnam

Minta's 1941 high school commencement program.

Mary Sue and W. E. Parmenter in the backyard of the family home in Throckmorton.

The women in Kappa Phi Social Club. Minta is seated second from the right in the first row.

Minta as a young teacher standing by the school building.

A 1959 issue of The Kennel, *the school newspaper.*

Walter Cypert.

Swimming at Cisco in 1947–48. (Minta is standing, facing the camera.)

Dancing at the depot in 1956–57.

Minta with students in the library during study hall.

Some of the students from business classes serving in the Commercial Club. Left to right: Pete Hitch, Jenny Liles, Jamie Nichols, Valene Shaw, and Minta Cypert.

Preface

Chapter One

Potts, Charles Shirley. *Railroad Transportation in Texas.* Bulletin of the University of Texas, No. 119. Humanistic Series, No. 7. March 1, 1909. Austin: University of Texas Press, 1909.

Merriman, Walter. *Once Upon a Time in Throckmorton.* Private printing, 1996.

Leffler, John. "Throckmorton County." *Handbook of Texas Online.* Published by the Texas State Historical Association. Accessed February 11, 2013. http://www.tshaonline.org/handbook/online/articles/hct05.

"Throckmorton, TX." *Handbook of Texas Online.* Published by the Texas State Historical Association. Accessed February 11, 2013. http://www.tshaonline.org/handbook/online/articles/hjt06.

Chapter Two

Werner, George C. "Texas and Pacific Railway." *Handbook of Texas Online.* Published by the Texas State Historical Association. Accessed February 11, 2013. http://www.tshaonline.org/handbook/online/articles/eqt08.

"Impact, TX." *Handbook of Texas Online.* Published by the Texas State Historical Association. Accessed February 11, 2013. http://www.tshaonline.org/handbook/online/articles/hni05.

Pirtle, Leota Nash. *Look Back with Pride, Look Forward with Hope: A History of the Throckmorton Methodist Church.* Nortex Press, 1976.

Waters, Ethel, with Charles Samuels. *His Eye Is on the Sparrow: An Autobiography.* New York, 1951; reprinted by Da Capo Press, 1992.

Chapter Three

Internet Movie Database. http://www.imdb.com.

Myers, James M. "Camp Barkeley." *Handbook of Texas Online.* Published by the Texas State Historical Association. Accessed February 10, 2013. http://www.tshaonline.org/handbook/online/articles/qbc02.

Leffler, John. "Throckmorton County." *Handbook of Texas Online.* Published by the Texas State Historical Association. Accessed February 11, 2013. http://www.tshaonline.org/handbook/online/articles/hct05.

Chapter Four

IBM Archives. *The Typewriter: An Informal History.* http://www-03.ibm.com/ibm/history/exhibits/modelb/modelb_informal.html.

Wikipedia. *Shorthand.* http://en.wikipedia.org/wiki/Shorthand.

CPSIA information can be obtained at www.ICGtesting.com
Printed in the USA
BVOW03s1317171113

336481BV00006B/15/P